Constance Fenimore Woolson

The University of Georgia Press

Athens & London

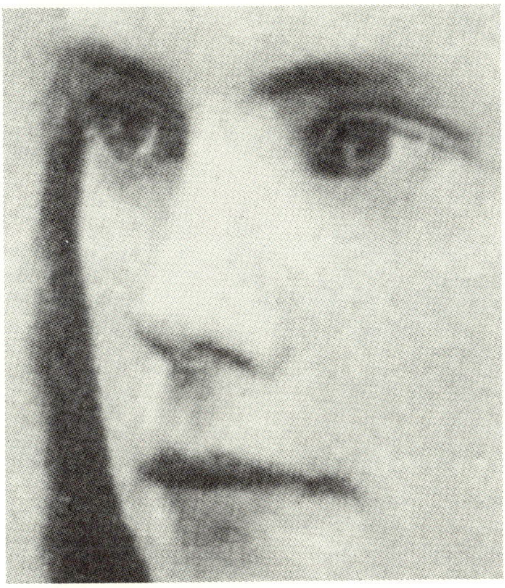

Constance Fenimore Woolson

THE GRIEF OF ARTISTRY

Cheryl B. Torsney

Athens, Georgia 30602

Designed by Louise M. Jones
Set in 11/14 Goudy Old Style
The paper in this book meets the guidelines for permanence and durability of the Committee on Production Guidelines for Book Longevity of the Council on Library Resources.
Printed in the United States of America

93 92 91 90 89 5 4 3 2 1

Library of Congress Cataloging in Publication Data
Torsney, Cheryl B.
Constance Fenimore Woolson.
Bibliography: p.
Includes index.
1. Woolson, Constance Fenimore, 1840–1894—Criticism and interpretation. I. Title.
PS3363.T67 1989 813'.4 88-17399
ISBN 0-8203-1101-4 (alk. paper)

British Library Cataloging in Publication Data available

Earlier versions of portions of chapters 1 and 3 appeared in chapter 7 of *Patrons and Protégées: Gender, Friendship, and Writing in Nineteenth-Century America,* edited by Shirley Marchalonis.

for Jack and Benjamin

CONTENTS

Constance Fenimore Woolson

INTRODUCTION

Throughout my research I have had to repeat and spell Constance Fenimore Woolson's surname, even for many of my erudite and eclectically read colleagues. "Not Wolfson, *Wool*-son: W-O-O-L." In a note to me, even the G. Pierpont Morgan Library, which holds Woolson's correspondence to Dr. W. W. Baldwin, originally spelled the name *Wilson* before correcting the error. The Fenimore everyone catches, of course, and asks about a relationship to the writer Mark Twain lampooned in his famed "Literary Offenses" essay. Alert to the currency of her matrilineal middle name, Woolson herself played it for economic gain. When her novels appeared in England, the by-line read "By a Niece of Fenimore Cooper," although Woolson was technically a grandniece. Her comment was "Isn't that 'Yankee' enterprise for an English firm?"[1] When I verify the relationship, my colleagues, Twain lovers all, sigh: "Sure hope she didn't write like he did."

If anyone recognizes Woolson for herself, it is a Henry James scholar. As a graduate student I found my interest piqued when I learned of a possible romance between James and Woolson. But what of his obscure hurt, the injury that exempted him from serving in the Civil War, I wondered. Who was this woman, other than the person whom many say served as the model for May Bartram in "The Beast in the Jungle"? Did she have a life of her own unconnected to that of "John Marcher," one of the stuffiest of literary prigs, a man who buys birthday gifts because, as he acknowledges, it makes him feel good about himself? One must do more than a modicum of research to discover that the answer to that question is a convinced yes. In the recent criticism, Alfred Habegger calls Woolson "one of the best of the novelists on the border between local color and realism," and many agree that important reevaluative work is yet to be done.[2] Other readings of Woolson treat her as a minor local colorist, interesting for her vivid descriptions but lacking in realism and excitement. She is more or less a curiosity, a descendant of Cooper, a companion of James, and a late-nineteenth-century spinster/scribbler. If we dig deeper, into the earlier appraisals, however, we will find a different picture of Woolson. There she is, if not revered, at least greatly admired, a popular and critical success.

My opportunity to find out more about this shadowy woman, who appears in the literary histories like May Bartram, facing the fireplace with her back to us, came in an NEH Summer Seminar directed by Elaine Showalter. She and the seminar participants helped me to focus my attention on Woolson's artist figures and their position in the development of the female *Künstlerroman* of the late nineteenth century. I owe these colleagues, especially Shirley Marchalonis, a great debt of thanks for their friendship as well as for their intellectual support. Following the completion of the seminar, the Delta State University Committee on Institutional Research funded my travel to collections holding Woolson's letters and memorabilia in Cleveland, Ohio, and Winter Park, Florida. By far, however, the American Council of Learned Societies and West Virginia University have been the most generous in their encouragement of my work, having furthered my research with grants and with reductions in my teaching responsibilities.

Special thanks go to a number of other friends and colleagues for support in bringing this study to publication: to Elizabeth Makowski, my editor at the University of Georgia Press, for believing in both Woolson and me; to Leslie Mitchner at the Rutgers University Press, for fostering my study of James and Woolson early on; to G. Douglas Atkins, for encouraging my research in critical theory; to Elizabeth Ammons, for making discerning and helpful comments on a late draft;

to Dennis W. Allen and Beth Daniell, for taking precious time during the last weeks of the semester to read the final draft of the manuscript for continuity; to Timothy Dow Adams, for providing moral support; to Kathleen J. Reich of the Rollins College Archives Department, for securing photographs of items from the Woolson Collection of Memorabilia for reproduction in this book; to Miriam K. Brock and Sherry Fox, expert readers and typists, for taking special pains with the physical manuscript; to Rebecca R. Loomis, for helping with the proof. Without the collaboration of all of these people, this book would never have been realized. The faults remaining with this, the "ill-formed offspring of my feeble brain," are, however, all my own.

My research into the life and letters of Constance Fenimore Woolson has raised many issues, beginning with her life as a daughter, a woman, and a writer in the late nineteenth century. I have taken a women's culture approach to answering the questions that have presented themselves. According to Elaine Showalter, such a theory "incorporates ideas about women's body, language, and psyche but interprets them in relation to the social contexts in which they occur."[3] That is, I have eschewed a strictly formalistic approach in favor of a contextual reading of Woolson's life and letters. That seems to me the most reasonable method to take when engaging in the first efforts at secondary study, especially for women writers, who as artists did not have the luxury of divorcing themselves from various less platonic demands on their time: children, husbands, housework, health. We as readers and critics must see them in their physical, moral, and legal environments. Supported by a foundation of sociocultural information, I have then asked a few biographical questions: Who was Constance Fenimore Woolson? More important, how did she perceive herself and her relationship to her editors, readers, and literary friends, such as Henry James?

All of these questions are prefatory to several larger ones, ones that are the center of my discussion regarding the development of the *Künstlerroman* among women writers in nineteenth-century America. I discuss that tradition as a prelude to the central issue of this study: the artist heroines of Constance Fenimore Woolson. These sharp women, always marginal to society, show up early in Woolson's fiction, in several of her first published stories, and continue as regular characters through one of the last stories she wrote, "In Sloane Street," a narrative about an American woman in England, who, in the course of the action, makes a pilgrimage to George Eliot's grave. I investigate the nature of the woman, of her art, and of the multiple conflicts her position as both woman and artist poses. I investigate the tension she must have lived with and the crises of identity society enforced on her. Her prototypical figure is often a creative artist—a musician, a painter, most frequently a writer—but sometimes she is a less traditional creator, weaving instead a fiction of self for others, as is the case with "The Lady of Little Fishing" and Madame Carroll in *For the Major.*

My conclusions will revolve around the question of "The Grief of Artistry," the subtitle of my study. For Constance Fenimore Woolson and for her heroines, artistry brought grief, as shown most clearly in her best story, "'Miss Grief.'" That grief is the grief of silence, of having something important to say and then having it suppressed either because society does not want to hear the message itself or because the message is being communicated by a woman. In such a way the woman artist is doubly marginalized.

The study is designed to respond, in a way, to Woolson's question to the writer and editor E. C. Stedman, "Why do literary women break down so," a query prompted by Elizabeth Stoddard's illness.[4] It is also written to suggest that the artists in Constance Fenimore Woolson's work—and Woolson herself—grief-stricken or no, are harbingers of heroines to come.

ONE • TRADITIONS OF ARTISTRY & GENDER: FICTIONALIZING THE JAMES-WOOLSON RELATIONSHIP

The lack of recognition given the name Constance Fenimore Woolson, even among new feminist critics and those well versed in women's fiction of the nineteenth century, is unfortunate. In her own day Woolson was a popular success: her publisher, Henry Harper, offered to pay her an additional thousand dollars and a royalty for her novel *Anne* (1882) because of its runaway sales.[1] Unlike some of the earlier women "scribblers," she was a critical success as well: Henry James wrote in 1884 that she was the only English-language novelist he read besides William Dean Howells. In her 1890 essay "Women in American Literature," Helen Gray Cone, characterizing Woolson as "robust, capable, mature," remarked that "women have reason for pride in a representative novelist whose genius is trained and controlled, without being tamed or dispirited."[2] Woolson's influence was apparently felt in the highest publishing circles, and she has been mentioned as possibly the person who opened the pages of *Harper's* and other literary magazines for Southern writers in an era when, according to Jay B. Hubbell, Northern magazines were regarded by

Southerners as "distinctly hostile" to Southern talents.[3] When she died in Venice in 1894, a probable suicide, she was widely mourned, and the weeks following her death brought eulogies in newspapers and magazines, often accompanied by an illustrated portrait.[4] (The one in *Harper's Bazar* occupied a full page.)

Woolson's writing continued to be admired and anthologized through the twenties. Fred Lewis Pattee in *The Development of the American Short Story* (1923) declares that "During the 'seventies undoubtedly she was the most 'unconventional' feminine writer that had yet appeared in America," but he also offers an opinion of her limitations: "Not in many ways was she significant; in some important details she was actually a retrogressive force. She never wholly outgrew, for instance, the earlier lessons she learned from her first enthusiasm, Charlotte Brontë."[5] Arthur Hobson Quinn, in *American Fiction: An Historical Survey* (1936), approves of Woolson's style, commenting that James's "judgment was sounder than that which has apparently forgotten her," and that when she died she was known as "one of the most consummate artists in that great epoch of the novel."[6] He cites Bret Harte as her major influence, although George Sand and George Eliot are mentioned far more frequently in her letters and journals. By 1948, although he still reviews Woolson's achievement favorably—he characterizes her tone as sensitive and delicate, her style as Jamesian—Alexander Cowie classifies Woolson as a "superior minor writer who is periodically 'rediscovered' by a sensitive critic or a zealous historian."[7] The two critical biographies of Woolson (Kern, 1934, and Moore, 1963) attempt to reclaim her, yet no work to date has been completely successful.[8]

Women's studies scholarship has resurrected the spirit of Constance Fenimore Woolson insofar as she is now included in biographical dictionaries of women writers; however, her work, when it is assessed, is still judged using a male-dominated critical bias akin to that used by Pattee in 1923, when he attributed Woolson's insignificance to her failure to outgrow her love for Charlotte Brontë. Lyon N. Richardson, in 1940, apologizes for Woolson in a typically patriarchal way:

> Her memories of girlhood were sensitive, but only from girlhood's point of view, and one is left with the distinct impression that the daughter-father

relationship was more adequately realized in her fiction than that of the daughter-mother. She was careful to choose heroines who were not beautiful, but who possessed some distinction of personality. There is sorrow and abnegation on occasion, but her wives are frequently self-centered and purposeless, whom the men would have done well to avoid. Briefly, nobility is lacking in a number of her characters for the very reason that the basic ambitions, interests, functions, and fruitions of life are lacking. But in the matter of frustrations her novels are psychologically interesting as studies of certain feminine classes: widows both young and old, young wives not engaged in establishing families, elder unmarried sisters, and spinsters.[9]

We find, however, Evelyn Thomas Helmick's judgment of Woolson harder to swallow, especially since it appears in a collection entitled *Feminist Criticism: Essays on Theory, Poetry and Prose:* "Such unattractive, if not improbable, martyrs are perhaps part of the reason Miss Woolson's work is seldom read today. The problems with her books are undoubtedly those characteristics which made them popular in her own day. Her characters, in exercising a restraint admirable to the Victorian mind, seem wooden and unreal: the endless feminine analysis of emotions and motivations becomes comic after a while; the plots become too circumstantial to bear."[10] Such an assessment hardly jibes with that of Helen Gray Cone in the last century. Clearly a new context is needed not only to put these evaluations in perspective but also to recognize the continuing worth of Woolson's writing for women's literary traditions.

What has happened to Woolson's reputation? Why is it that a writer who was numbered among the country's best has been forgotten? Is it because her work does not deserve to be remembered, that her interest and value have dissipated with the passing of time? The explanations are multiple.

The disappearance of Constance Fenimore Woolson from our literary histories and so from the classroom may lie in an accident of birth: she comes of age as a writer just after the heyday of domestic fiction (her first sketches are published in various magazines in 1870) and dies in 1894 just before the maturation of the New Woman. Thus, her professional career is interposed between two periods when women wrote from positions of secure identity and power. The women of the first half of the nineteenth century grew up in an integrated and rich homosocial culture reinforced by the bonds of womanhood.[11] Their fiction, often moralistic in tone, celebrated their culture by casting as a protagonist one of its worthy products: "a heroine who, beset with hardships, finds within herself the qualities of intelligence, will, resourcefulness, and courage sufficient to overcome them."[12] This domestic fiction continued in vogue until just after the watershed of the Civil War.

The next great watershed was not only the actual turn of the century but also the anticipation preceding its arrival. Behind the bounding baby of 1900 were New Women urging it forward, impatient for its first tottering steps. These women rejected the earlier formulations of the "women's sphere," for the power they sought for themselves existed outside the pale of the domestic environment. Defying those roles in which she had always been cast, the ideal New Woman became educated and earned her own living.[13] She was strong and healthy and believed in the strength and health of her independent views. As Carolyn Forrey notes, "Above all, she wanted to stand in a new relation to man, seeing herself as a companion—an equal—rather than as a subordinate or dependent."[14] The professional as well as the personal world of the new woman writer (and her heroine) was heterosocial rather than homosocial as the world of her mother and grandmother had been.

At least two decades, however, intervened between the weakening of the bonds of womanhood and the freedom of the New Woman, and it is in this twilight world that local color writing comes to the fore. The Civil War and its attendant destruction and impoverishment of life and land had altered the American psyche irrevocably. Ann Douglas Wood affirms that the war served as the major catalyst for local color writing:

> Partly as a result of the war, women were breaking into other professions, most notably medicine, and it was in controversial areas like this, rather than the realm of literature, that the battle for increased freedom for women was principally being fought. Hence, fewer rebellious feminine spirits were turning to the literary life as the logical outlet for their ambitions. Indeed, for the

women Local Colorists, the act of writing offered an exercise in nostalgia or a release for despair rather than a vehicle for a covert power play. . . . If they are proud of anything, it is of their passionate commitment to the rear guard.[15]

As the ties of a strong, domestic, largely urban network dissolved with the advent of modern technology (of which the Civil War was a manifestation) and with the opening of the frontier, the voice of the woman writer, who saw her world as attenuated and impoverished, began to be heard. Without the traditional networks to support (and to tie) her, she had to create her own identity from the available possibilities and find her way in the world the best she could. Wherever she was—in New England, in the Midwest, in the South, or even exiled in the Old World—she existed on the frontier of traditional femininity. With this breakdown of women's culture and the means of disseminating women's fiction, the literature of the local colorists was co-opted by male-dominated periodicals, such as the *Atlantic, Harper's, Lippincott's,* and *Appleton's,* and so institutionally marginalized.

Constance Fenimore Woolson presents a classic case of the literary artist whose fiction has slipped into the abyss of powerlessness that lies between two dominant generations. Within this gulf local color or regional writing flourished. More than any other form of women's writing, local color fiction has remained the most neglected and understudied. It has been perceived as a short, secret passage between the great halls of romance and realism, or, to change the metaphor, if the novel is a Moby Dick in a turbid sea of symbol, the local color story is a five-cent goldfish in a tank at Woolworth's: domestic, picturesque, yet happily ephemeral. Because local color chose the short story and the sketch over the novel as the preferred genres of expression, many take the shorter forms less seriously. But as Judith Fetterley notes, "nineteenth-century American women found it easier to write well in forms that appeared less literary, artistic, and serious."[16] Indeed, Woolson's best work is in short rather than long fiction.

For some, "local color" has taken on a perjorative hue. Leon Edel, for example, has difficulty rationalizing Henry James's inclusion of an essay on Constance Fenimore Woolson in his *Partial Portraits* (1888):

"For Miss Woolson was on the whole rather prosy and banal, a journeywoman of letters. . . . Her work is minute—and cluttered; she is an ardent devotee of 'local color.'"[17] Although some, notably Josephine Donovan and Ann Douglas Wood have attempted to do justice to the fiction of postbellum women, women's local color writing has been overlooked by many feminist critics in favor of earlier domestic fiction and later post-suffrage writing.[18]

As in any traditional society, the artists of each group served as spokeswomen for the values of their worlds. For example, in Catharine Sedgwick's short story "Cacoethes Scribendi" (1835), the inhabitants of an almost exclusively female society write merely for entertainment rather than from pretentions to artistry, but when the group's great young hope marries the town's Prince Charming, "they relinquished, without a sign, the hope of ever seeing her an AUTHOR."[19] The moral: authorship (read art) is no substitute for marriage, even for a budding artist. At the other end of the spectrum is the New Woman artist as exemplified by Mademoiselle Reisz, the concert pianist in Kate Chopin's *The Awakening* (1899), who lives in the heterosocial world of turn-of-the-century New Orleans. Edna Pontellier remembers her idol's characterization of the artist's position in the world: "The bird that would soar above the level plain of tradition and prejudice must have strong wings. It is a sad spectacle to see the weaklings bruised, exhausted, fluttering back to earth."[20]

In ways we might expect but have thus far failed to recognize, the artist figure in local color writing also serves as the quintessential example of her female type. Out on the geographic, social, cultural fringe, and most often, as Ann Douglas Wood has shown, husbandless and childless, the artist of local color fiction stitches herself a gown from remnants, but once in it, alters it to something else. She recognizes her artistry and demands recognition, but caught as she is historically, between homosocial domesticity and the heterosocial commercial world, she exists in an unenviable transitional space among gender roles, social roles, and cultural roles.

Her fictional artists suffer similar frustrations in attempts to create their identities. In discussing contemporary female writers, Judith Kegan Gardiner in "On Female Identity and Writing by Women," states that "the woman writer uses her text, particularly one centering on a female hero, as part of a continuing process involving her own self-definition and her empathic identification with her character."[21] The same is true for the earlier writers of domestic and New Woman fiction, but Gardiner's assessment of the female writer's motives is particularly true of the writers of what has been termed local color fiction, and so of their artist figures: writers, painters, musicians. For, as Gardiner concludes, "'The hero is her author's daughter.'"[22] Struggling with their identities as people and as artists, local color writers (and their artist figures, it is understood) are in powerless positions, as opposed to writers of domestic and New Woman fiction. This may help to explain the mysterious lack of recognition given Woolson.

Alice Hall Petry offers another theory to explain the strange disappearance of the once-famous Constance Fenimore Woolson from literary consciousness. "Part of Woolson's decline is due," she reasons, ". . . to the simple fact that she 'existed,' as it were, only in her writings rather than as a distinct personality. She did not painfully explore her inner life, as did Adams in his *Education;* nor has she been granted an exhaustive psychobiography, as has James in Leon Edel's multivolume analysis."[23]

Edel's biography of James provides, in fact, the most accessible of the available Woolson biographies, and most readers who recognize her name do so because of Edel's exhaustive research. His recognition of Woolson's role in Henry James's life is, however, a mixed blessing. For although he is to be commended for raising the issue of the writers' relationship, he is primarily responsible for perpetrating the legend of the lonely spinster who carries a torch for the icy James all over Europe. Despondent over her rejected attentions—James was her better and only paid her visits out of kindness, so the story goes—Woolson threw herself out of her second-story window on that winter day in Venice. A guilty James resurrected her in the character of May Bartram in "The Beast in the Jungle."

Such is the fiction penned by Edel, who asks point-blank, "Had her act been a partial consequence of frustration—of frustrated love for Henry?"[24] Edel writes that in the four extant letters from Woolson to James "she plays the woman scorned and the woman pleading; full of self-pity at her footloose state. . . . Their tone, above all else, however, is one of despair and of a touching loneliness—a middle-aged woman reaching out to a man younger than herself."[25] (Edel misleads his reader here: Woolson was, in fact, only three years older than James.) Throughout their correspondence, Edel claims, Woolson casts herself in the role of the "rejected woman."[26] The picture he draws is of a desperate, lovesick, she-novelist, no longer a cub, nipping at the heels and thereby embarrassing the exalted lion. In relying on the stereotype of the rejected woman, Edel betrays his bias.

It seems clear that James and his contemporaries would not have assented to Edel's portrait of Woolson as "on the whole rather prosy and banal, a journeywoman of letters. Without style, and with an extreme literalness."[27] Professor Edel assumes, wrongly I believe, that James's praise of Woolson's writing in his *Partial Portraits* essay is disingenuous, motivated by "loyalty and friendship" rather than by sincere and simple admiration for her achievement. "The final impression can only be that he is honoring Fenimore's dedication to letters less than her devotion to himself," Edel asserts.[28] Given James's opinion of the high responsibility of the critic, however, it is unlikely that he would praise Woolson unless he meant it. As he declares in his review of Rebecca Harding Davis's novel *Dallas Galbraith,* the critic "must be before all things clear and emphatic. If he has properly mastered his profession, he will care only in a minor degree whether his relation to a particular work is one of praise or of censure."[29] Moreover, if James's purpose were to feign for the public, why would the private man write to Howells that Woolson was the only English-language novelist he read besides his friend? Why would James, in a letter to his brother William three years after his correspondence with Howells, call Woolson "the gifted authoress"?[30] For James, Woolson exemplifies woman writing in the late nineteenth century, and in her portrait he speaks of her in the same breath as he speaks of Mesdames Sévigné, de Staël, and Sand.[31] She is to be admired.

Not only James himself but also his sister, Alice James, valued Woolson's fiction. In fact, Katharine Loring, Alice's companion, had been reading Woolson's story "Dorothy" to Alice just before James's sister died.[32] Alice James and Woolson were longtime friends, the writer frequently visiting the invalid Alice. Woolson also corresponded with Katharine Loring "about everything from recipes for baked beans to Ruskin" to medical school education for women; apropos of the latter, Woolson insisted that the two sexes be educated together.[33] The feminine mind, she asserts, "has been kept back, & enfeebled, & limited, by ages of ignorance, & almost servitude."[34] Alice offers the negative of Edel's snapshot of the James-Woolson relationship, presenting her brother as an attached admirer in a letter to her brother William ("Henry is somewhere on the continent flirting with Constance") and later to her Aunt Kate ("Henry has been galavanting on the continent with a *she*-novelist; when I remonstrated he told me he thought it a 'mild excess.' ")[35]

James's frequent references to Woolson in letters to friends contradict Edel's assertion that James rarely mentioned the depth of his "virtuous attachment" to others.[36] In a note to John Hay at Christmas 1886, James writes that their "amiable and distinguished friend Miss Woolson . . . dwells at five minutes' distance."[37] He continues to say that they meet every day or two, frequently dining together. A few months later he describes Woolson to Grace Norton as "an excellent woman, of whom I am very fond, though she is almost impracticably deaf."[38]

Because he and Woolson shared their friendship with fellow expatriates Francis Boott and his daughter Lizzie, their neighbors in Florence, the group banded together in their grief when Lizzie died. In a letter to the mourning father dated 29 October 1888, James writes that he talks of Lizzie with Woolson, whom he's been visiting for ten days; several months later he reiterates Woolson's regard for Lizzie's memory.[39] In nearly every letter to Boott, whose song Woolson quotes in "Dorothy," James mentions their mutual friend. On 9 March 1892 James writes: "Our poor Fenimore, at Oxford, which she likes, has had a very painful illness—an affection of the head, brought on by trying *false drums* (a new invention) in her ears. But she is better, though her hearing isn't. I go to see her next week."[40] In fact, just before Woolson died, James wrote to Boott that he was preparing to "pay a visit to our excellent friend Fenimore . . . I figure her as extremely exhausted (as she always is at such times), with her writing and re-writing of her last novel—a great success, I believe, in relation to the particular public (a very wide American one) that she addresses. She is to have, I trust, a winter of bookless peace."[41] At her death, James, horrified and depressed, wrote of his wild emotions to at least six different people: Dr. W. W. Baldwin, Rhoda Broughton, John Hay, Francis Boott, Katherine DeKay Bronson, and William James. This is not the response of a man hounded by a woman, but rather of a friend who has lost a companion with whom he shared both professional and personal interests.

The legend of the spinster's chasing the lion over a continent is further mitigated by an examination of Woolson's other correspondence. It is important for us to understand that the tone Edel catches in Woolson's letters to James—paradoxically assertive and simultaneously self-effacing but always effusive concerning her correspondent's latest work—is the same tone she employs in her letters to others whose work she admires: E. C. Stedman, John Hay, and Paul Hamilton Hayne.

To clear things up, or at least to bring them into better focus, given the distorting glasses of history and literary criticism, much of what Edel reports is verifiable. Constance Fenimore Woolson, holding a letter of introduction from Minny Temple's sister, Henrietta Pell-Clark, met Henry James in April 1880. (Edel embellishes the truth, I think, when he writes that she arrived in Europe "half in love with James.")[42] The two writers got along splendidly, corresponded religiously (Woolson told James that she wrote to him mostly to entertain herself), and visited each other frequently.[43] During these visits they walked, toured galleries, and dined. In 1887, in fact, James and Woolson lived in separate apartments of the Villa Brichieri in Florence, and, as his letters detail, they met in several European capitals in the years following, once discreetly selecting hotels on opposite banks of Lake Geneva. Certainly Henry James must have admired Constance Woolson and enjoyed her intelligent humor enough to have been despondent over her death.

The documented details of her probable suicide are few. Early in the morning of 24 January 1894, Woolson rang for one of her servants at the Casa Semitecolo to fetch her some warm milk. On returning, the retainer found Woolson in a crumpled heap on the pavement below her second-story window. Her favorite gondolier carried her unconscious body back to her bedroom, where she soon died. John Hay handled the funeral arrangements, and Woolson, like Daisy Miller, was buried in the Protestant cemetery in Rome. Reasoning the death a suicide, James, Edel presumes, refused to attend the funeral. Several months later, however, James volunteered to accompany Woolson's niece to the writer's sealed rooms to conclude her aunt's affairs and, Edel asserts, to see that Woolson had kept her vow to burn his letters after reading them. Once granted access to her things, James could also have destroyed any other papers that might have been interpreted as incriminating.

James's reading (or at least Edel's text of James's reading of Woolson's death) is a convention-laden male fantasy. In that sexist romance the dependent woman prefers not to live at all if she can't have all of her man. Although we have reason to believe that Woolson threw herself to her death rather than falling in an influenza-induced delirium as others have speculated, she was most likely not prompted by unrequited love for Henry James. Rather, evidence of a philosophical consideration of suicide, coupled with hereditary (patrilineal) depression, postpartum-like stress (she had just finished *Horace Chase*) and financial worries, implies that issues more important than Henry James convinced her to take her own life at age fifty-three.

Woolson's books and letters suggest why she may have committed suicide. First, in her personal copy of *The Teaching of Epictetus* she has both bent down page corners and marked the sections justifying suicide with vertical pencil lines down the adjacent margin.[44] A particularly significant paragraph in the chapter "On Solitude" is marked in the inside as well as the outside margin with a double line. It reads: "And when, it may be, that the necessary things are no longer supplied, that is the signal for retreat: the door is opened, and God saith to thee, *Depart.*"[45] The chapter note to this passage is also marked with a double line and is especially pertinent since it condones self-annihilation in the face of being unable to await "God's time": "But the Stoics taught that the arrival of this time might be indicated by some disaster or affliction which rendered a natural and wholesome life impossible. Self-destruction was in such cases permissible, and is recorded to have been adopted by several leaders of the Stoics, generally when old age had begun to render them a burden to their friends."[46]

Woolson's letters to all of her regular correspondents, E. C. Stedman, her nephew Samuel Mather, and John Hay, are shot through with references to illness and attending depression, their onslaughts and retreats. She is ill for months, even entire seasons at a time, with influenza, inner ear problems (which her doctor diagnoses as neurotic), and various other ailments. In a letter begun on 10 December 1888 but spanning several weeks, she considers her health at that time of year newsworthy for its stability: "I am quite scandalously well this winter. Have'nt had an ill moment; & am stout as can be. I am so much better—my health so much *firmer*—than it used to be that it is really quite remarkable. (I was ill last winter; but that was owing to mental depression.)"[47]

Depression was Woolson's nemesis. In a letter of 23 July 1876 to E. C. Stedman, she had explained: "I am overweighted with a sort of depression that comes unexpectedly, and makes everything black. My grandfather gave up to it and was a dreary useless man; my father battled against it all his life, and again and again worried me about it; but I was young then, and only half believed in it. Now, he is gone, and it has come to me. I try to conquer it and sometimes I succeed, sometimes I do'nt" (Stedman Papers). In a letter to her girlhood friend Arabella Carter Washburn, she again acknowledges that she suffers the same fits of depression her father had: "Don't fancy I am sad all the time. . . . But at times, in spite of all I can do, this deadly enemy of mine creeps in, and once in, he is master. I think it is constitutional, and I know it is inherited."[48] Her recurring malaise becomes even more pronounced whenever she finishes a project, resembling postpartum depression. In a letter to Katherine Mather she writes that the effort of writing a novel "takes such entire possession of me that when, at last, a book is done, I am pretty nearly done myself."[49] When we now read the letter James wrote to Boott only weeks before Woolson's death, in which he wishes her a quiet winter recuperating from the completion of her last novel, we can only smile bittersweetly at the irony.

In tracing the fluctuation of Woolson's moods and health, I have found her depressions to be most severe in midwinter, when daylight hours are short, suggesting, perhaps, seasonal affective disorder (SAD), which Jack Fincher calls "a baffling depression whose cyclic onset appeared to be curiously governed by the changing length of the day."[50] In fact, Woolson's references to illness and depression increase considerably during the autumn and winter months. January seems to be the cruelest month for her; May brings relief. Summer and early fall letters are filled with reports of day trips, long walks, outdoor adventures. In a letter of 2 March 1882 Woolson writes to her niece of her strange, cyclical health: "My health amuses me a good deal, because it is so absurd. Every year proves to me more and more decidedly that it is entirely a matter of warmth. As long as it is warm, really warm and not any make-believe of it, I am well, remarkably well; the instant it becomes cold, I am wretched. Sometimes the wretchedness takes one form, sometimes another. Sometimes a doctor would give it this name; sometimes that. But the point is that the minute it is warm, all the wretchedness, no matter what serious and dignified name it may have borne, vanishes into nothing, and never comes back until the weather is cold again" (Mather Family Papers). Although her health may have appeared to depend on warmth, it could conceivably have also depended on the associated sunlight.

The shorter days of fall and winter may have convinced Woolson that, at the age of fifty-three, her life, too, was waning. In her letters preceding her death, we see her dwelling more and more on what she considers her advanced age. On 20 November 1893, just two months before her death, she writes to Samuel: "But one must do, from day to day, the best one can. And my 'infirmities' are upon me now; they will not grow worse. (This last sentence means that your aunt is already pretty old!) I hope you will not be shocked if I add that for a long time my daily prayer has been that I may not live to be old; I mean really old" (Mather Family Papers). Three days later, in a short note, she admits that she feels "old, & tired, & indifferent" (Mather Family Papers).

Woolson's sense of helplessness and hopelessness had been accelerated, undoubtedly, by her feeling that she was running out of both time and money. Throughout her years in Europe, Samuel Mather had her power of attorney in America and oversaw his aunt's finances; thus, many of her letters to him concern the drawing of bank drafts and the sale of property. During the last three years of her life, however, her worry about money grew, and her letters reflect an increasing desperation as she feels her lifetime dream of retiring to a quiet Florida cottage slip away. In a letter posted from Cairo and dated 17 April 1890, Woolson writes that although she is enamored of the Holy Land, she cannot allow herself to stay the summer: "No; if I am to get my finances into shape, I *must* give myself to steady work, in the most quiet & unexciting place I can find" (Mather Family Papers). Two years later, on 8 February 1892, she composes another letter in the same key. (I quote from it extensively, as much to make available that "distinctive personality" which Alice Hall Petry thinks missing from our literary histories as to demonstrate Woolson's growing nervousness over the constraints of time.)

> To have done with the blue part first, let me say that I am still suffering from the pain which attacked me a month ago. But it is now much less severe, so that I bear it better. (I have not much fortitude about pain, you know!) The English doctor here, a clever young man, thought the whole affair was neuralgia. "Neurotic" was his word; that is, a malady of the nerves of the head. I did not, in my heart, agree with him. And I think it is *now* pretty well decided that it has been a slow gathering in the inner ear, first on the right side; & now on the left. I say "inner," because there has been no sign of anything *visible* any where. The first two weeks I let the thing run on, with a few remedies of my own. But the intense pain forced me to send for a doctor, & though he has accomplished nothing else, he has given excellent prescriptions for sleeping-draughts, so that I get through the nights. To day, as yesterday, I am putting on linseed poultices every 15 minutes, & in spite of a low state of depression, my reason tells me that in all probability in a few days more, this left-side ache (or rather stab) will be over, & well, just as the right side now is.—The loss of time preys upon me most of all. I try not to think of it. I read & read. And when I no longer do that, I even play solitaire! If you & Flora could have peeped in half an hour ago, and seen me seated on the rug, with the kettle on a trivet attached to the grate behind me, & all the materials for the linseed poultices assembled on a tray at one side, while I, with tear-stained face, was drearily playing solitaire on an atlas propped on

my knees, you would have laughed, I am sure. I never play games you know; so when I play solitaire, it is desperation indeed.

Later in the letter Woolson responds to her nephew's request that she spend the summer with him and his family at Newport:

I can't come this summer simply because every well moment *must* be given to finishing the novel which begins in a serial in Harper's Magazine next December. I have already postponed it a whole year, owing to the tiresome condition of my health; never really ill, I may say, sadly enough with truth, that for a year I have not been really well. Unless I wish to make the Harpers lose all patience with me, I must keep my engagement fully & promptly this time. (Mather Family Papers)

Finally, on 20 November 1893, she asks Sam to sell one of her bonds and send her one thousand dollars to cover the expenses of setting up housekeeping at the Casa Semitecolo. "I have made the necessary first purchases; and now, having settled myself for a while, I find I am beginning to be haunted by the fear that my reserve fund at the Bank here is not large enough to leave me free from immediate care" (Mather Family Papers).

Personal philosophy, depression, illness, age, and worry all probably combined to lead Constance Fenimore Woolson to commit suicide. Early in her career, in a letter of 23 July 1876, she had written to E. C. Stedman, asking, "Why do literary women break down so. . . . It almost seems as though only the unhappy women took to writing. The happiest women I have known belonged to two classes; the devoted wives and mothers, and the successful flirts, whether married or single; such women never write" (Stedman Papers). Recently Elaine Showalter has cited "an increase in psychosomatic illnesses and stress diseases" in women writers of Woolson's era, resulting from tension over their identities. This generation, Showalter observes, is the first in which female suicide becomes a trend.[51] Woolson's choice to take drastic means to end her life places her firmly in the women's literary tradition. Although Henry James was a close friend, it seems that his guilt over her death, as represented by Leon Edel, probably resulted from an inflated view of his role in her life.

The standard reading of Woolson's death, which I have tried to unravel, begins to suggest how her life and her writing have always been marginalized, have always been read as secondary to James's. Her life, for example, has been seen as the inspiration for much of James's fiction after her death, following the traditional master-disciple pattern. Edel, for instance, cites Woolson as the real-life May Bartram and suggests that James's sense that Woolson had betrayed him inspired "The Altar of the Dead."[52] Moreover, he writes, evidence demonstrates that "Fenimore had a certain exalted notion of her own literary powers. She aspired to the style, the manner, the mastery of Henry James," but she could never attain to the Jamesian literary laurel.[53]

Woolson's works have been read, even by her champions, as the ash from which the Jamesian phoenix rises. Sharon Dean astutely notes that "The Beast in the Jungle" springs from an entry in Woolson's notebook: "To imagine a man spending his life looking for and waiting for his 'splendid moment.' 'Is this my moment?' 'Will this state of things bring it to me?' But the moment never comes."[54] "Old Gardiston," a Woolson story that predates by twenty-one years *The Spoils of Poynton* (written close on the heels of Woolson's death), features a climactic conflagration; "The Figure in the Carpet," the title of the James story, is a phrase from Woolson's notebooks; Woolson's "A Transplanted Boy" tells of a child's rejection by adults, much like James's "The Pupil"; and Tita, the sister of Anne in Woolson's first successful novel, is the original name of Tina in "The Aspern Papers."[55]

This study attempts to regain for Constance Fenimore Woolson the respect she has been denied, in part because she is perceived as an acolyte of Henry James: first by placing her within the context of nineteenth-century women's culture and writing; and then by taking up a particular figure she employs throughout her career, the artist-heroine. The artist-heroine becomes for Woolson the representative of the best sort of woman, for she attempts, against all odds, to assert her individuality through art. That art takes many forms—music, painting, literature, modeling of a physical self—yet it seems clear that Woolson is nearly always talking about narrative.

Her artist figures are destined to suffer, however, for their attempts to usurp the male power of creative artistry. If the patriarchy takes them seriously, they will be silenced by humiliation or other subversive measures. If not, they will be made to feel inadequate and be married off, their beings appropriated by their husbands. In the world of formal creative artistry, they can never attain to any power or position; however, they may exercise their artistry on themselves, turning their own bodies into texts that reflect the grief of powerlessness. Or, as spinsters, they may turn their lives into artistic texts of self-sacrifice.

Woolson herself suffered the grief of artistry: the peculiar, powerless situation of a woman writer in the last quarter of the last century. Lacking self-confidence, she asked male friends to intervene on her behalf with publishers. When she sold well, her publishers required more from her than she could produce. And now, in the last half of this century, her talent, like that of her characters, is considered "prosy and banal," important only for the inspiration she provided Henry James.

On the contrary, Constance Fenimore Woolson was a perceptive writer who understood the task of female artistry and the suffering it was bound to produce; a sensitive woman who recognized her precarious, powerless position in a changing world. Her artist-heroines reflect that sad knowledge.

TWO • A WOMAN WRITER BORN MIDCENTURY

To begin then, who is this woman who has been so ill-treated by literary historians? The easiest way to describe her is as a woman writer born midcentury. That is, Constance Fenimore Woolson suffered from being born into a complex matrix of cultural circumstances: first, she grew up in a world where the True Woman (1820–60) was losing ground but before the New Woman (beginning in the 1880s) gained prominence; second, even though she came of age in a women's culture, in her later life she lacked enduring relationships with other women outside her immediate family, depending instead on the emotional support of male correspondents, such as her friends Henry James, E. C. Stedman, and John Hay, and her nephew, Samuel Mather.[1] In any case, Woolson was a literary and an emotional exile, from the women's world of home and hearth, living first in Cleveland, Ohio; then in the South; then abroad, far from the New England literary community where women's friendships, like that between Sarah Orne Jewett (born the same year as Woolson) and Annie Fields or between Woolson's friends Alice James and Katharine Loring, would become legend. Woolson's accident of birth and her own personality, resulting, in part, from her being born between generations of women with strong identities, may begin to explain why Woolson has been given only a passing nod in many literary histories and is still completely absent from others, for example, *The Norton Anthology of Literature by Women.*[2] Raised as a True Woman, believing, despite herself, in many of the cult's values, she also identified with the New Woman's agenda. Finally, Constance Fenimore Woolson could find a home in neither camp.

Woolson was born into a conservative if adventurous family with strong New England roots, a family whose women would have belonged to the Cult of True Womanhood, women who would have raised their daughters to accept their values. As Barbara Welter notes, the phrase was used "as frequently as writers on religion mentioned God"; however, an exact nineteenth-century definition is unavailable since the parameters of the cult were assumed by writers and readers, speakers and audiences.[3] Welter, nonetheless, attempts to define the attributes of True Womanhood using four qualities the True Woman was expected to demonstrate to herself, her husband, and her community: piety, purity, submissiveness, and domesticity.[4] This True Woman, ever attentive to her husband and family, maintained her most important relationships, however, with other women, living a female-bonded life of love and ritual.[5]

From her own birth, Woolson, like others of her sex who attended both the newly born and newly dead, was intimately connected with both birth and death. Only three days after baby Constance's arrival in 1840, scarlet fever struck the Woolson household, killing three of the infant's older sisters. This devastating event marked Woolson's entry into the world. Her two older sisters died while the budding writer was a young teenager, leaving Constance the eldest sibling.[6]

Her young life was typical of that of a middle-class girl born in the 1840s on what was becoming the quickly civilized frontier of the Western Reserve. Like her heroine Anne Douglas (and like Margaret Fuller in an earlier time), Woolson looked to her father, a former newspaper man, for her early intellectual training. From him, she had inherited her poor lungs, deafness, and mental illness. (Thus, when she wrote about the depression she had inherited from the Woolson family, she assigned it a male pronoun.) In her youth, Woolson's primary filiation, however, was with a strongly bonded female community of family and a few childhood friends, rather than with women who shared her growing professional and intellectual interests. Young Connie received the proper education of a girl on the Western Reserve, first enrolling in Miss Hayden's School in the 1840s and then attending the Cleveland Female Seminary in the 1850s, where she was taught by a recent graduate of Mount Holyoke College, Miss Linda Guilford, with whom she maintained a correspondence throughout her life. Woolson then attended and graduated from Madame Chegaray's French finishing school in New York City in 1858, after which her father took the family on a tour of the Eastern seaboard, where Woolson, according to her younger sister, Clara Woolson Benedict, made a great success.[7]

She remained a dutiful if eccentric young woman, working in a Union post office during the Civil War and caring for her mother and father, believing that a woman's glory was marriage. She declared herself, however, a "desolate spinster" while in her twenties, suspecting that marriage would threaten if not entirely destroy her close ties with a childhood friend, Arabella Carter.[8] In an obvious response to the announcement of Belle Carter's impending marriage, Woolson responded:

> There is no danger of my thinking of, and liking you less now that you are going to be married. But I have felt such a conviction that you would some day lose your interest in me, and also all outside things, that I thought best to prepare for the worst . . . I don't mean to say that you will ever come actually to dislike me, but you will probably take a middle course. You have been the best friend I ever had and have done and said countless kind things for me. *I* shall never change . . . and if, after all, things should not turn out as I fear, and "Mrs. Washburn" continues the same friend that "Belle" has been for so many years, don't you suppose I shall be glad and grateful? . . . I am *so, so* glad for you. A man's true, earnest love is a great gift. If you do not accept it and enjoy it, I shall—shake you! Why can't you fling all your misgivings to the winds and be simply happy? The glory of your life has come to you. Everything else is trivial compared to it.[9]

Such correspondence demonstrates the intensity of relationships in the female world of love and ritual and also Woolson's fear that that world on which she had come to rely was disappearing, as indeed it would.

Like other women of her era, Woolson continued to rely on her female networks and to identify strongly with the women in her family as she grew up. After her father's death on 6 August 1869, Woolson was her mother's primary caregiver, and the two women traveled south together every winter after having spent the summer at Cooperstown on Lake Otsego with her mother's Cooper relatives, a tradition she details in a short essay entitled "The Haunted Lake."[10] When Hannah Pomeroy Woolson died on 13 February 1879, her daughter was so bereaved that she could scarcely express her desolation. As she wrote to E. C. Stedman a month later on 14 March 1879, "The whole world is changed to me. The one person who loved me dearly has gone. Nothing,—nobody,—can ever fill her empty place" (Stedman Papers). The tragedy of having the family ties unknot before her eyes was multiplied when the last of Woolson's Cooper aunts died in 1891–92. Woolson identified strongly with them—with their New England sensibility and strength—and felt that with their passing, an era had ended in her life.

Woolson's female network furnished her with the companionship of her sister Clara Woolson Benedict and Clara's daughter, Clare, who lived with Woolson off and on during their trips to Europe, and also with an opportunity that would change, if not her life, then at least the way she has been remembered. This significant event took the form of a letter of introduction to the new literary celebrity who was to become her lifelong friend, Henry James, in the spring of 1880. Woolson had received the letter from an acquaintance, the older sister of James's favorite cousin, Minnie Temple.

Her social concerns, not only for filiation, but also for custom and domestic comfort, align Woolson with women's culture. At the same time, however, Woolson's discomfort in the role of woman of the house suggests the conflict she experienced between what she felt was expected of her and her actual sense of self. For example, unlike the True Woman, Woolson was never confident in her role as domestic engineer; she was not a particularly effective money manager, frequently writing to her nephew, Samuel Mather, requesting his intervention in banking problems. Although she realized that her finances were limited, she bought only the best. Her letters of 19 December 1884 and 7 June 1887 detail, first the impossibility of purchasing a curious Italian lucerne because the price, though not high for the market, overshot her budget, and second, her acquisition of new rugs and Christofle flatware (Mather Family Papers). She wrote to Mather that she absolutely had to have the new things to make her feel at home. In the style of the period, in the manner of the True Woman, she decorated with personal knickknacks, such as pillows and lace doilies, and with photographs of Howells, James, and Stedman, and elsewhere photographs of Meredith and Turgenev, declaring her filial piety.[11]

Dress, too, occupied a rather uncomfortable position in Woolson's life. Had she been a True Woman, she would have felt comfortable with adorning herself, with recognizing her ornamental nature. Fashion, however, was not Woolson's forte, but as the dutiful daughter that she was, she felt obliged to dress appropriately, consciously to resist affecting the appearance of a bluestocking. However, Woolson's insecurity regarding her dress is evidenced in many letters detailing her discomfort with the process of clothing herself suitably. In correspondence dated 20 January 1876 and 23 July 1876, Woolson acknowledges Mrs. Stedman's assistance in selecting and draping her gowns (Stedman Papers). Woolson further reveals in the latter missive that she has spent one hundred dollars, surely an immense amount for the time, on a new black grenadine, without the silk underskirt, only to discover that not only was the ensemble poorly constructed ("the long bones down the back [I don't mean my own exactly] have come out and the sleeves had come apart" [Stedman Papers]) but the other women were dressed in another fashion. She then jokes about joining the dress reform movement endorsed by New Women, a radical move that would have violated her upbringing but would have made dressing easier, for it necessitated, she writes, "one black alpaca."

Throughout her life Woolson was sensitive not only to her dress but also to her body, for she sensed that physically she had not been created in the image of the True Woman. She reports fluctuations in her weight in letters to various correspondents, using it as a measure of her health, yet she is never satisfied. At her top weight of 149 pounds, she is surely much heavier than she had been as the admired "slim girl" of Linda Guilford's letters. And like the *Harper's* publicity portraits and the Greenough sculpture, the medallion of Woolson cast in bronze by

American sculptor Larkin Goldsmith Mead reflects a pleasing countenance Woolson never thought attractive. Although her reservations and explanations concerning the various likenesses could leave one feeling that the lady protests too much, Woolson and the women of her day adhered to an image of ideal beauty to which Woolson did not conform although she was not at all unattractive. Her many protests regarding the ugliness of her "mug" undoubtedly resulted from insecurity in the face of the ideal blond-haired, blue-eyed angel of the house. For not only did Woolson not have a home, husband, and children; she also did not have blond tresses and a slim figure. She must have questioned her own femininity and felt that others impugned it, too.

Her home and her appearance were two things a True Woman must maintain, or so Woolson's upbringing had suggested. Her own adventurous spirit, her insecurity regarding her domestic capabilities and her perceived undesirability, and a rebellious streak, however, subverted that very world in which she had been reared, creating an ambiguous relationship with the women's sphere. Once again on the subject of marriage: "Family people appear to think that unmarried people are very self-indulgent because they want to amuse themselves. It does not seem to occur to them that they (the married) gave themselves the pleasures which *they* preferred. Let them bear, then, the accompanying cares, and not criticize those who refrained from such ties."[12]

Even as Woolson lived her life trying to emulate the dress and behavior of the True Woman as much as she could, given her individualism, her sensibility resembled that of the next-generation New Woman. Like the True Woman of two generations before, the New Woman was a generalized abstraction, a type whose personality was understood as standing on the bedrock of independence. As Carolyn Forrey explains: "The New Woman was self-reliant. She was determined to live her own life and to make her own decisions. She was eager for direct contact with the world outside her home. She held independent views. Often she managed to be financially independent as well, earning her own living and perhaps committing herself to a lifelong career."[13]

Many of Woolson's views express New Womanhood ideals even though Woolson herself was a child of the True Woman ethos. For example, she is radical in her opinions of women's education and of women's literature as a result of that lack of education. Europe she views as a bad place for very young ladies, who, since they have no freedom, are forced to remain young longer, like so many Pansy Osmonds.[14] Any such premeditated inhibition of maturity is near criminal for Woolson: "Girls do so need a more thorough education! I never hear, or, rather, I seldom hear, one of my own sex talk long without noticing the lack of broad, reasonable, solid views. . . . But I am sure that education is all that is required. I do not think the feminine mind inferior."[15] Without the training, however, the feminine mind is uncritical. Woolson laments: "Many women, good women, think scenes in certain novels and plays, 'So untrue to nature!' These are the women who live always in illusion! They believe in all sorts of romances which have never had the least actual existence."[16] Women, she insists, do write and are able to appreciate the finest writing. For when E. C. Stedman discusses Mrs. Browning as a lesser mind, Woolson is incredulous. Her special admiration, though, is for George Eliot: "From first to last, she did exactly as she pleased—law or no law, custom or no custom!"[17] In that praise we see the conflict that plagued Woolson: though independent and able to live as she wished, she nonetheless felt bound by the proprieties of, as she put it, law and custom.

This conflict is neatly allegorized in an anecdote Clara Woolson Benedict, Woolson's sister, relates in recounting the family's tour of the Boston seaside resorts following Constance's graduation from Madame Chegaray's School:

> But the literary talent in her led her to do things that those *not* thus gifted, did not do. Mother often said to her: "Connie, do not carry an inkstand up and down stairs as you do—you will some day fall and injure yourself, and spoil one of your pretty new dresses!"
>
> So one day the fall came, and I saw it! Connie was not injured; she had on a lovely grey costume, very becoming and beautifully made—she started to come down the steep hotel stairs, holding a portfolio . . . and on the top of the limp portfolio stood her ink bottle with no cork in it! She stumbled and went down and the whole bottle of black ink poured over this lovely dress![18]

If we read the inkspot on the lovely dress as a metaphor for the fate of the woman in the woman writer, we can understand how Woolson's world (and in many ways, Woolson herself) saw literary ambition—the ink—as a stain on the pretty frills of feminine consciousness.

The conflict between Woolson's upbringing in a society where the ideal woman was the often not-too-worldly light of the home and her middle-age existence in the more androgynous New Woman world is illustrated particularly by Woolson's own perception of herself as an artist. On the one hand, she is embarrassed when an editorial she wrote for her sister's father-in-law, George Benedict, then editor of the *Daily Cleveland Herald,* was picked up by other papers and her name is printed all over the country.[19] This publicity she traditionally views as improper and unfeminine, and in fact, her first story appeared under the pseudonym of Anne March.[20] At the same time, however, she insists on her identity as a writer, telling her childhood friend Arabella Carter: "I want you to think of me not as your old friend, when you read my writings, but as a 'writer,' like anyone else."[21] She identifies herself particularly with George Eliot, writing a poem praising her and declaring apropos of *Adam Bede:* "whatever one does must be done with one's might and I would rather be strong than beautiful, or even good, provided the 'good' must be dull."[22] In the same vein she writes: "I have such a horror of 'pretty,' 'sweet' writing that I should almost prefer a style that was ugly and bitter, provided it was also *strong.*"[23]

Woolson's notebooks include topics for characters and situations that reflect the conflict in her life between her domestic upbringing and her more modern tendencies. Among the topics suggesting her conservative childhood are the following entries:

> To imagine a girl (or woman) doing some extraordinarily brave and heroic action, and then immediately afterward being afraid of a mouse.
>
> A love story, told in the first person, written down to exorcise it perhaps, on a New Year's night in an old Italian villa. Or on the last night of the old year. It tells how she loved him. He did not think of her at all; in fact he never noticed her.
>
> An imaginative girl with deep feelings falls in love with a man of the

artistic temperament. She sees in him noble gifts, noble tendencies and aspirations. But every one else sees in him only his dangerously-pronounced and overshadowing qualities. She loves him, but he cares nothing for her.[24]

These ideas sketch the ambivalence about ambition, love, and art evident in the fiction of Woolson and many of her contemporaries. In each narrative possibility, female potential is limited by an implied male world. The last description in particular presents a potential artist-heroine who, perhaps because of gender restrictions, must project her own ambitions onto a lover who is unworthy of them.

Other entries concern women who live on the boundaries of traditional womanhood and who are thus marginalized by the patriarchal society: a divorcée, a woman who sets out to ruin a man, a woman with good taste who revolts against "the sordidness of her lot," a woman with imagination, a lady who commits a crime, a misunderstood woman.[25] These women, who exist outside any community, have an experience similar to Woolson's own. In a letter dated 13 February 1876, Woolson writes to Paul Hamilton Hayne: "I spoke of myself as a 'Philistine,' because I do not seem to belong to anybody, or any class. The Boston writers, young and old, hang together; the New York journalists and magazine people have their own creed; and the southern, ditto. Whenever I hear any of those people talk, or receive letters from them, I perceive this.—Then, much of the praised literature of to day, and all days, *I* do not like; another 'Philistine' trait!"[26]

Henry James was on target in his assessment of Woolson and her simultaneous insistence on her professionalism and her deference to male expectations when he wrote that she had a conservative nature, "that for her the life of a woman is essentially an affair of private relations."[27] In "Miss Woolson," James himself verges on boldly stating the very problem with Woolson's reconciliation of career and gender:

The work of Miss Constance Fenimore Woolson is an excellent example of the way the door stands open between the personal life of American women and the immeasurable world of print, and what makes it so is the particular quality that this work happens to possess. It breathes a spirit singularly and essentially conservative—the sort of spirit which, but for a special indication pointing the other way, would in advance seem most to oppose itself to the introduction into the feminine lot of new and complicating elements. Miss Woolson evidently thinks that lot sufficiently complicated, with the sensibilities which even in primitive ages women were acknowledged to possess; fenced in by the old disabilities and prejudices, they seem to her to have been by their very nature only too much exposed, and it would never occur to her to lend her voice to the plea for further exposure—for a revolution which should place her sex in the thick of the struggle for power. She sees it in preference surrounded certainly by plenty of doors and windows (she has not, I take it, a love of bolts and Oriental shutters), but distinctly on the private side of that somewhat evasive and exceedingly shifting line which divides human affairs into the profane and the sacred. Such is the turn of mind of the author of *Rodman the Keeper* and *East Angels,* and if it has not prevented her from writing books, from competing for the literary laurel, this is a proof of the strength of the current which to-day carries both sexes alike to that mode of expression.[28]

In a manner akin to that of earlier women writers, Woolson employed conservative strategies in dealing with her publishers and editors. For her, being a woman writer meant not pressing issues of title, length, or compensation on her own behalf but rather working through powerful intermediaries. Like many other women of her century, Woolson relied on her friends to get for her what she wanted from her publishers, including contracts and raises. Specifically, Woolson looked to E. C. Stedman, who talked Horace Gilder, editor of *The Galaxy,* into publishing Woolson's writing, for Woolson profusely thanks Stedman and then asks him in a letter dated 12 June 1874 to use his influence in the cause of another publication, the short story "Jeannette" (Stedman Papers). Another letter, this to Henry James, may imply that he intervened with the Harpers in increasing Woolson's royalties for *Anne,* though we cannot know for certain that such was the case.[29]

Her identity, especially in these situations, was compromised, for Woolson saw herself both as a woman (in a letter to James she portrays herself as an "admiring aunt"[30]) second to men in all things, and also as a literary personality, for whom literature is a career. She must, for example, keep up on all of the magazines while she is abroad so that she does not miss a rising trend in her chosen profession. Like the scribbling women of the earlier part of the century, writing was her livelihood; however, unlike the members of that earlier generation, Woolson consciously saw herself as an artist, particularly concerned with issues of realism, as she demonstrates in a long letter dated 9 January 1893 to Samuel Mather regarding the credibility of Horace Chase's speech in that eponymous novel (Mather Family Papers).

Woolson's membership in this Lost Generation, however, is not strictly attributable to her date of birth, for other women writers of the era did not feel alienated from the literary establishment and have been, in effect, canonized in recent revisions of American literary history. On the whole, however, the writers who have found their way into (or back into) the program of literary studies had access to the literary machine of their day either through their families or through other relationships. Most of the recently canonized nineteenth-century American women have been New Englanders: Margaret Fuller, Sarah Orne Jewett, Mary Wilkins Freeman, for example. (The most striking exception to this rule is, of course, Kate Chopin: she, however, was championed in the early sixties by a male critic.)

Scholars who seek to subvert the "Lost Generation" argument for Woolson's disappearance do cite the case of Sarah Orne Jewett, who, we must remember, was a lifelong resident of New England, the seat of literary power, and close friend of Annie Fields of the Ticknor and Fields publishing house. Others point to Alice James, whose diary has been recovered in part because of an interest in the dynamics of her famous family and whose friendship with Katharine Loring has been viewed, like Jewett and Fields's relationship, as a perfect Boston marriage. Woolson, however, was a lifelong resident of nowhere. Although born in New Hampshire, she was reared in Cleveland, vacationed in upstate New York and in the Midwest, and lived in the South and in Europe. Her writing and her life can be seen, in fact, as presaging the rootlessness and the alienation thematized in modern literature rather than the ethos of women's community as exemplified in a work like *The Country of the Pointed Firs*. Unlike Jewett but like most women, Woolson was ignorant of the politics of publishing. And unlike Alice James, who lived in Europe for reasons of preference, Woolson lived abroad to economize.

It has been said that Woolson has not found her place in the new literary histories because she lacked the encouragement of a strong, extended women's network. This argument seems to assert that she is absent because the facts of her life and writing do not fit our new paradigm of the nineteenth-century woman writer bonded to other women. On the contrary, although she corresponded frequently with males, these letters and others reveal close ties with her mother, her sister Clara, and her nieces Clare and Kate, as well as passing friendships with many other women, including Frances Hodgson Burnett. Perhaps one of the other reasons the reconstructed canon has been slow in admitting Woolson is precisely that her life, one of exile and loneliness abroad, does not mirror our new definition of the nineteenth-century woman writer. Living in an age when women's friendships are valued, we somehow do not want our new models to be writing, as Woolson does on 28 September 1874 to E. C. Stedman, "If women would ever say what they mean I should like them better. As it is I am afraid of them; afraid of their 'ridicule-behind-one's-back,' I mean" (Stedman Papers).

The fully realized characters in Woolson's artist fiction often take on Woolson's own fragmented identity, rehearsing both her transitional generational position and her individual history of family disaster and exile. Woolson's artist-heroines can neither entirely align themselves with the Cult of True Womanhood nor fully reject their upbringing, join the dress reform movement, and become New Women. Their dilemma, one of loneliness and longing, and of the powerlessness derived from a divided sensibility, is registered—by Woolson and her fictional artists—in their art.

THREE • *ANNE:* WOOLSON'S PORTRAIT OF A LADY

Woolson's transitional position—on the one hand a member of the "scribbling" sorority, on the other an exile who isolated herself from society in order to devote herself to art—is best demonstrated, perhaps, by example. Woolson's earliest stories are reminiscent of the earlier fashions in women's writing discussed so thoroughly by Mary Kelley and Nina Baym, among others.[1] For example, the early piece "Duets" (1874) features two friends, Olive and Helena, who get what the other wants in a husband.[2] And although "Weighed in the Balance" (1872) takes up women's suffrage as a topic during a lake voyage—one gentleman believes that only when men recognize their "soul-companions . . . will woman reach her apotheosis" and "human intellect, embodied in the clear crystals of woman's mind, rise to its true place," while another maintains "that love is her power, and we love her, not for her mind, but rather for her heart"—a quiet girl, in the manner of a domestic romance, saves the day when a sudden storm threatens the outing.[3] In "The Lady of Little Fishing" (1874), the opening story of Woolson's first collection of short fiction, *Castle Nowhere: Lake Country Sketches,* a beautiful spiritlike woman civilizes a rough logging camp, and in "Old Gardiston" (1876) a vanquished Confederate belle finds herself in love with a Yankee officer, happily capitulating to him in the end.[4]

To demonstrate further Woolson's debt to the women fiction writers who preceded her and to highlight her own internalization of women's culture, it is instructive to consider her first long work and most popular piece of fiction, *Anne.*[5] By reading the novel in terms of another novel of the period, Henry James's *The Portrait of a Lady,* we will see even more clearly how Woolson used the earlier women's fiction tradition in order to find a voice and how she later adapted it to make statements about the possibility for women's artistry in her world, about the powerless position of female artists in a patriarchal culture.[6]

My purpose here, however, is not to create more anxiety by arguing influence. I see neither Woolson nor James as derivative: both are part of the same textual fabric. Rather, I think it more valuable to examine how, as a result of their shared cultural milieu, they focus on similar themes yet produce gender-inflected results. Whether or not, like Alfred Habegger, we see James as an effeminate "sissy," he is still a man writing from his own gender perspective.[7] Likewise, Woolson is a woman writing from hers.

Both Henry James's and Constance Fenimore Woolson's first important novels were published serially, his in the *Atlantic* (from November 1880 to December 1881) and hers in *Harper's New Monthly Magazine* (from December 1880 to May 1882). Both are novels of love and marriage, a theme as old as the genre itself. Both *The Portrait of a Lady* and *Anne* present female protagonists akin to the prototypical women's heroine whose characteristics, "intelligence, will, resourcefulness, and courage," have been outlined by Nina Baym.[8] Isabel Archer and Anne Douglas are provincial orphans who are adopted by eccentric aunts after the deaths of parents with whom the aunts had argued. Both young women make a successful entry into society after being taken in by their relations, and both marry men of questionable virtue. In each character's case another man, Ralph Touchett and Gregory Dexter, respectively, at some point provides for the heroine's material well-being. Although the novels share structural similarities and a relation to the Ur-plot of trial and triumph as elucidated by Baym, they are based on different gender assumptions, traditions, and development.

Carren Kaston has defended James against the charges of some hostile feminist criticism by noting that "James wrote regularly with a profound sensitivity to what it was and very often still is like to be a woman."[9] Although, as Alfred Habegger asserts, James was "in sympathy with the best feminine values," he was nonetheless male, still on the outside.[10] Still, his effort to understand is genuine, his understanding as certain as possible. From his own hegemonic position, he presents a woman of imagination who, because of the constraints of the male world in which she lives, cannot realize the triumph of that imagination. As Kaston puts it, "Such independence to which Isabel at first aspires is unattainable not only because of the existence of others, who constitute society and exert pressure on her, but because of conditions within Isabel herself."[11] It is Isabel's tragedy that she cannot really act independently. She can only be managed. As James writes, "Madame Merle had married her" (430). Even grammatically Isabel is an object, not a subject. She is passive, not active, as a male culture expected a woman in her place to be.

Keys to Isabel's failure lie in her own habits of mind, habits born of reading two classes of literature: romances by and about women and texts from the transcendentalist tradition. These two sources of Isabel's ideas suggest what Kaston calls her "conflicting attitudes toward power: her desire for self-origination on the one hand and, on the other, her attraction to dependency."[12] Isabel (as well as James, of course) is not at fault; rather, as Kaston puts it, "given the powerlessness women frequently feel, the challenge of self-origination could not easily be met by any woman, even one as generously conceived as Isabel is by James."[13]

From the beginning Isabel understands her world in textual terms. On her arrival at Gardencourt, she is thrilled to meet Lord Warburton: "Oh, I hoped there would be a lord; it's just like a novel!" she gushes (27). Indeed, in the following flashback to Lydia Touchett's visit to Albany to fetch her niece, Isabel is ensconced in the library, where she reads indiscriminately, "guided in the selection chiefly by the frontispiece" (33). Her reading includes "the London *Spectator*" and "the latest publications" (41–42), both of which would have treated women's issues. Other evidence demonstrates, however, that Isabel has been reading romantic women's novels as well. These unnamed novels help to set up her expectations only to have reality decimate the tenderly held images.

Mr. Touchett, sensing Isabel's impending disaster, raises the issue of the discrepancy between fantasy and reality in women's fiction, but Isabel either does not hear or does not heed the warning. Their discussion begins with Isabel's wondering whether English character confirms what she has read in books. Her uncle replies that he is unfamiliar with what appears in novels, that he believes only what he has learned from firsthand experience. But Isabel continues to push the question of novelistic representations of reality by asking how she will be treated in society. "I don't believe they're [the English] very nice to girls; they're not nice to them in novels" (58). Daniel Touchett's response might have served to warn Isabel, but finding herself in a situation usually reserved for novels, her ears are deaf to her uncle's warnings.

> "I don't know about the novels," said Mr. Touchett. "I believe the novels have a great deal of ability, but I don't suppose they're very accurate. We once had a lady who wrote novels staying here; she was a friend of Ralph's and he asked her down. She was very positive, quite up to everything; but she was not the sort of person you could depend on for evidence. Too free a fancy—I suppose that was it. She afterwards published a work of fiction in which she was understood to have given a representation . . . of my unworthy self. . . . Well, it was not at all accurate; she couldn't have listened very attentively. . . . I don't talk like the old gentleman in that lady's novel. . . . I just mention that fact to show you that they're not always accurate." (58–59)

Isabel might have taken to heart James's ironic joke about people who think that novels faithfully record experience, but she does not. Throughout the early sections of the novel, she reads real-life situations according to women's writing conventions: she sees Warburton "as a hero of romance" rather than as a troubled man caught in a changing political order and his home "as a castle in a legend"; she has read that the English "are at bottom the most romantic of races"; she identifies herself as a young woman being made love to by a nobleman in a "deeply romantic" situation (66, 75, 77, 96). When Henrietta Stackpole tries to penetrate Isabel's novelistically clouded vision by asking her "Don't you know where you're drifting?" Isabel replies: "No, I haven't the least idea, and I find it very pleasant not to know. A swift carriage, of a dark night, rattling with four horses over roads that one can't see—that's my idea of happiness." Henrietta responds that her language sounds like that of "the heroine of an immoral novel" (146).

That Isabel uses such language should come as no surprise since she understands her world in part through the filter of the romance tradition of women's novels. As William Veeder observes, Isabel talks a conventional line, using the extravagant language of women's fiction. Like women's heroines, she relies "upon the pretty set-speeches conventional with pretty heroines."[14] Her own naive reading deceives her and tricks her into marriage with a man whose name, Gilbert, suggests the heroes of romances written by both Sir Walter Scott and Susan Dudley Warner.[15] At the end, still following the literary convention of her romance novels, Isabel is left with only one way out, self-sacrifice. Ironically, it has been another convention of women's fiction, the sickly, feminized Ralph Touchett, himself a writer (and reader) of the genre, who prepared Isabel for her downfall when he convinced his father to provide for the requirements of his cousin's imagination, thus authoring the pre-text of her disaster.

But the romance tradition is not the only literary tradition that fails Isabel. When Mrs. Touchett first meets Isabel in the family library in Albany, the girl has been "trudging over the sandy plains of a history of German Thought" (34). She takes to heart the superiority of the male virtues of logic, reason, and mind over the female ones of emotion, sensitivity, and heart. Had she been conscious enough to note that her reading was indicting her own character, she might have become a resisting reader, recognizing that the texts she was reading made her own gender into the enemy.[16] Isabel's transcendentalist reading tricks her into believing in the possibilities for her own independence, possibilities reserved, according to the American tradition of idealism, for men. Emerson, one of Isabel's heroes, for instance, as Joyce Warren notes, was "unable to see women as individuals like himself." "It is clear that his philosophy [of self-reliance and insistence on high goals] was not intended to apply to women."[17] In the beginning of the novel Isabel is the embodiment of the Emersonian idealist: she believes in the world "as a place of brightness, of free expansion, of irresistible action" (54); she believes in "the continuity between the movements of her own soul and the agitations of the world (41). But Isabel is a woman, as James well knows—as Kaston remarks, "Isabel Archer is more than incidentally female."[18] Her reading of a male intellectual philosophy does not serve her. As she laments: "She had desired a large acquaintance with human life, and in spite of her having flattered herself that she cultivated it with some success this elementary privilege had been denied her" (431). The "privilege" is denied her because of her sex and her goodness, and both the reader and James mourn her lost opportunity.

Thus, Isabel's naïveté fails her on two levels. First, she thinks the world of the romance novel real, allowing it to dictate experience to her, revealing her dependency; second, she thinks male transcendentalism and idealism written for her, thus revealing her paradoxical desire to write her own text of self. James does not condemn the romance vision itself; however, he thinks that the tradition of German-Concord transcendentalism was responsible for Isabel's naive perception of reality and for her failure to allow her imagination free rein. But finally, Isabel, as a woman in a man's world, a woman written by a man (sympathetic though he be), can only respond as she does: as a mostly passive participant whose glorious imagination will never experience free rein though it may triumph over some of the obstacles it confronts.

Nearly three-quarters of a very long letter from Woolson to James, dated 12 February 1882, is taken up with her criticism of *Portrait.* By far the most telling of Woolson's responses to the novel is the whole of her last paragraph:

> How did you ever dare write a portrait of a lady? Fancy any woman's attempting a portrait of a gentleman! Would'nt there be a storm of ridicule! . . . For my own part, in my small writings, I never dare put down what men are thinking, but confine myself simply to what they do and say. For, long experience has taught me that whatever I suppose them to be thinking at any especial time, that is sure to be exactly what they are *not* thinking. What they *are* thinking, however, nobody but a ghost could know.[19]

Woolson, of course, is making a mild joke, and, in fact, she does attempt several portraits of gentlemen, both in her last novel, *Horace Chase,* and in "'Miss Grief,'" a narrative told from a male first-person perspective. Yet, just as James's *Portrait,* though about a woman, presents a heroine from a male tradition where women, even admirable, imaginative ones, are in a sense forcedly passive, Woolson's narratives featuring male characters evolve from the women's writing tradition we see described, for example, by Nina Baym in *Woman's Fiction* and by Mary Kelley in *Private Woman, Public Stage.*[20] In this tradition the female character is active, not passive; the protagonist is the writer's alter ego rather than a female character for whom the male author has a large degree of sympathy. In a letter dated 30 August 1882, Woolson compares her work to James's:

> All the money that I have received, and shall receive, from my long novel, does not equal probably the half of the sum you received for your first, or shortest. It is quite right that it should be so. And, even if a story of mine should have a large "popular" sale (which I do not expect), that could not alter the fact that the utmost best of my work cannot touch the hem of your first or poorest. My work is coarse beside yours. Of entirely another grade. The two should not be mentioned on the same day. Do pray believe how acutely I know this. If I feel anything in the world with earnestness it is the beauty of your writings, and any little thing I may say about my own comes from entirely another stratum; and is said because I live so alone, as regards to my writing, that sometimes when writing to you, or speaking to you—out it comes before I know it. You see,—I like so few people! Though I pass for a constantly smiling, ever-pleased person! My smile is the basest hypocrisy.[21]

That her writing cannot compare to James's is undeniable: hers is the writing of a woman, as the passage abundantly demonstrates. It is cautious, modest, self-effacing, yet the turn at the end, the suggestion of wearing a mask, even in comparing her work with his, is reminiscent of a familiar strategy used in American women's writing since the time of Woolson's sister New Englander Anne Bradstreet. Like her letter to James, Woolson's writing employs women's writing traditions, such as the writer's identification with her heroine and the widespread use of feminine archetypal patterns and images; and like the domestic writings from the earlier part of the century, Woolson's works empower women in many ways rather than lament their powerlessness in the outer world while compensating them with an imaginative inner life.[22]

Anne, the novel about which Woolson wrote to James, is the first of her strong women narratives. It was printed in several editions during her life, again after her death, and just recently with a new introduction.[23] Although past critics have praised *Anne* primarily for its local-color descriptions of Mackinac Island, Michigan, many agree that because the novel is replete with issues of self-identity, it deserves renewed attention. The issue of identity is the same one James treats in *Portrait,* yet since male and female definitions of identity and power differ, the thread is spun out with differing tension by male and female writers.

One of the ways that male and female texts differ is in the identification of the writer with the protagonist. Isabel is not James, nor was she meant to be, and Woolson teases James about his attempt to paint the portrait of a woman. Anne, however, is in many ways Woolson herself, substantiating Judith Kegan Gardiner's hypothesis that a woman writer "uses her text, particularly one centering on a female hero, as part of a continuing process involving her own self-definition and her empathic identification with her character. Thus, the text and its female hero begin as narcissistic extensions of the author."[24]

Anne Douglas and Constance Fenimore Woolson share interests and background, not the least of which is the name *Anne,* which Woolson adopted as a pseudonym for her first publication, *The Old Stone House* (1872). Both Anne and Woolson were New Hampshire natives and as children spent periods on the upper peninsula of Michigan, where a memorial to Woolson with the name *Anne* at the head of the tablet was erected in 1916. Both young women, though accomplished in the liberal and fine arts, protest that they are ugly. Woolson's portraits and her descriptions of Anne, however, belie such evaluation. Perhaps as a reaction against her sense that she falls short of the American ideal of beauty, Woolson develops a love of letter writing, the art of communicating without being seen. Anne shares that love. Just as Woolson tells James that she writes to him for her own amusement, Anne, in writing to her fiancé, Rast Pronando, finds that through the use of language she may assert a control over her life. (It is, on the other hand, the workings of language in literature that represent Isabel's inability to control her life.)

Both Woolson and her textual daughter also assert power and identity in physical activity and exertion. Throughout her life Woolson rowed to release energy as well as to pass a pleasant Saturday afternoon. Near the end of *Anne,* the heroine uses rowing as a release and as a means of coming to terms with her identity. In addition to rowing, Woolson loved any sort of physical activity, especially walking, and her letters are filled with references to hour-long morning jaunts and afternoon treks of six to eight miles. The place of physical exercise in Anne's and Woolson's lives is reflected in Ellen Moers's reading of walking as a recurring pattern in women's writing, signaling feminist independence and drive.[25]

Woolson's use of archetypal patterns and images in women's writing further identifies her (and *Anne*) with the women's writing tradition, gaining for Woolson depth and power. Among the archetypes Woolson's novel uses in some fashion are those of the green world epiphany (the coming to self in nature) and the green world lover (the coming to passion in nature), both elements of the archetypal feminine *Bildungsroman* as discussed by Annis Pratt. As Pratt explains, in nature, the stage for growth, activity, and confirmation of self-identity, women find "solace, companionship, and independence."[26] An important distinction is to be made here: for the transcendentalists (and for Isabel) nature is intellectualized, as evidenced by the analytic presentation of the subject in Emerson's famous "Nature" essay. Nature is a representative force rather than a fundamentally real part of our lives. In women's writing, however, nature is a personified friend. In the female *Bildungsroman* the girl takes possession of herself in taking possession of nature. Anne loves the trees so much she talks to them. Like her heroine, Woolson feels most independent and powerful—most herself—out in nature.[27]

The green world is the most important setting in Woolson's novel. In a culminating scene, Anne recognizes her friend's killer and is thus empowered to exonerate her lover through knowledge gained while rowing on a lake. In another of her green world epiphanies "among the arbor vitae, where there was an opening, like a green window overlooking the harbor," Anne agrees to marry young Rast Pronando, after his near drowning (132). But Rast is not Anne's green world lover. That figure, associated with the mythic dying god, appears in the person of Ward Heathcote, whose surname is Woolson's adaptation of another famous woman's green world lover. She retailors a rather wild, uncivilized Heathcliff into a more civilized, well-bred Heathcote. A Union captain in the Civil War, he is wounded in West Virginia, and, nearly dead, is restored to life by Anne.

In the archetype, the restorer is a goddess: Aphrodite, Ishtar, or Isis. Anne, in fact, is endowed with similar mythic resonance tying her to the power of the archetypes. From the second page of the narrative, Anne is described as "a young Diana," an allusion that reverberates throughout the novel. Both James and Woolson play on the allusion with their respective heroines; however, James's use is disguised in Isabel's last name, whereas Woolson's use is overt, appealing directly to the women's literary tradition of using goddess archetypes. James uses it from a male perspective to suggest Isabel Archer's female virtue, an abstract idea; Woolson uses it to suggest Anne's physical "vigor" and "elasticity," a concrete description. Their use of the references to Diana echoes their differing versions of transcendental nature: for James and Isabel it is intellectual; for Woolson and Anne it is sensate.

Anne, posed braiding her hair, is also called Ariadne, a figure as familiar as Diana in the women's literary tradition. Indeed, she is both: in her guise as Diana, she is the huntress who dwells alone in the woods and mountains; as Ariadne, she is abandoned by Rast Pronando. But Anne (Woolson) is also Ariadne, a weaver, a domestic maker of fictions, who grows in that capacity over the course of the novel. Early in her recognition that she enjoys writing, we are told that "she never put down any of her own thoughts, opinions, or feelings: Her letters were curious examples of purely impersonal objective writing." Woolson continues:

> Egotism, the under-current of most long letters as of most long conversations also, the telling of how this or that was due to us, affected us, was regarded by

> us, was prophesied, was commended, was objected to, was feared, was thoroughly understood, was held in restraint, was despised or scorned by us, and all our opinions on the subject, which, however important in itself, we present always surrounded by a large indefinite aureola of our own personality—this was entirely wanting in Anne Douglas's letters and conversation. (98)

Throughout the course of *Anne* the heroine's narrative talents grow until, at the climax of the novel, Anne demonstrates her new mastery of narrative form by weaving on the witness stand the fabric of truth, designed to acquit her lover. When the jury cannot arrive at a verdict, Anne rereads the text of the murder herself, discovering the killer. Finally, in the last pages of the novel, the passive voice of her early reflection on writing is rewritten in the active, identifying herself as the star of the show: "I, Anne, take thee, Ward, to my wedded husband, to have and to hold, from this day forward" (539). Unlike Isabel, Anne can assert her identity in the real world, as suggested by her new command of language. To the end, Isabel, given her circumstances, cannot vigorously and independently pursue her dream. She remains, in the last words she utters in the novel, an object, as she implores Caspar Goodwood, "As you love me, as you pity me, leave me alone!" (489).

Writing her own text of self and arriving at her own identity have not been easy for Anne. At every turn in the novel someone is attempting to appropriate her by stripping her of her linguistic being. Rast calls her Diana; Mrs. Vanhorn calls her Phyllis; Helen calls her Crystal (a particularly suggestive nickname since it implies a reflective relationship between Anne and Helen, one with a singularly complex inner composition and transparency); Miss Lois calls her Ruth Young. Her egotistical assertion at the end, "I, Anne," both defines her powerful new statement of identity and marks an assertion of Woolson's fictional power. Tied into archetypal patterns, that power strengthens the weave.

Before we leave *Anne* and the way it works with the women's literary tradition, we need to consider the function of Anne's half sister Tita. Much intrigued by the French-American half-breed with more than a trace of Indian blood, Henry James thought highly of Tita as a literary creation, as he writes in his *Partial Portraits* sketch of Woolson. That Tita "vanishes into the vague" after the reader has "built great hopes" on her is problematic, however.[28] What James does not understand is that Tita is a nineteenth-century women's literary archetype: the madwoman in the attic, or, in the case of *Anne*, the wild child on the island. She cannot be permitted any more narrative space than she has or she would take over. After fulfilling her purpose, she can be dispensed with.

Tita is the madwoman from the other side of the mirror Woolson holds up to herself in her projection of Anne. In *The Madwoman in the Attic* Sandra M. Gilbert and Susan Gubar describe the dynamics of such a mirroring:

> Even the most apparently conservative and decorous women writers obsessively create fiercely independent characters who seek to destroy all the patriarchal structures which both their authors and their authors' submissive heroines seem to accept as inevitable. Of course, by projecting their rebellious impulses not into their heroines but into mad or monstrous women . . . female authors dramatize their own self-division, their desire both to accept the strictures of patriarchal society and to reject them. What this means, however, is that the madwoman in literature by women is not merely, as she might be in male literature, an antagonist or foil to the heroine. Rather, she is usually in some sense the *author's* double, an image of her own anxiety and rage.[29]

Tita is truly Anne's mad double. Born of the same father (the same patriarchal structure) but of different mothers, Tita and Anne are both intimately related and decidedly divergent. Whereas Anne was born an Episcopalian in civilized New Hampshire, Tita is the Catholic daughter of his second wife, a French woman with Indian blood, whom he married in the uncivilized territory of the Western Reserve. Her religion, region, and language make Tita a dark unknown, a marginal Gothic figure from the very beginning.

Her personality reinforces her "otherness" vis-à-vis her older sister. While we first see Anne actively hanging Christmas wreaths at the church, Tita is "basking in the glow" of the fireplace, looking up listlessly (9). Anne's eyes are "wide open, and frank" (2), and the "adjective generally applied to her was 'big'" (3). Her heavy hair is demurely braided and pinned up in the fashion Woolson herself adopted. Tita, on the other hand, is "small—a strange little creature, with braids of black hair hanging down behind almost to her ankles, half-closed black eyes, little hands and feet, a low soft voice, and the grace of a young panther" (9). Anne has the blush of a peach, but Tita's complexion is pallid. Anne maternally cares for her half brothers; Tita threatens violence: "If you come any nearer," she tells one, ". . . I shall lay open the side of your head" (9–10). Tita rules the boys like a king, exhorting them with foul language and avenging herself against them for invading the privacy of her fur-carpeted lair near the fire:

> When they had been unbearably troublesome she stole into their room at night in her little white nightgown, with all her long thick black hair loose, combed all over her face, and hanging down round her nearly to her feet. . . . she left a lamp in the hall outside, so that they could dimly see her, and then she stood and swayed toward them slowly, backward and forward, without a sound, all the time coming nearer and nearer, until they shrieked aloud in terror, and Anne, hurrying to the rescue, found only three frightened little fellows cowering together in their broad bed, and the hairy ghost gone. (10)

Elsewhere, too, Tita is depicted as a ghost. On the same Christmas Eve that Anne hangs the wreath, Tita steals into the sitting room to examine the contents of her stocking. When she does not find the hair ribbons she wants, she writes a letter to Santa asking for them and puts it in her father's way. Her mission complete, she goes back to her own room "like a small white ghost" (23). Anne, innocent of Tita's machinations, provides the ribbons for her sister's pleasure after consulting with her father. Tita's ghostly image is a correlative for the "uneasy sense of trouble" that surfaces "like a veiled, formless shape" (20) whenever William Douglas thinks of Tita. "The sins of the fathers," he reflects.

Compared to both a cat and an embalmed monkey of the Nile, Tita at thirteen years old, neither child nor woman, is a preternatural, mythic, dangerous, mysterious force. She dresses entirely inappropriately for a Christmas dance in "a fantastic short skirt of black cloth barred with scarlet, and a little scarlet bodice" (33). When Tita is said to look like a circus rider in such a thin costume—the colors of blood and passion, we note—Anne confesses that she knew nothing of her sister's plan to dress in such an outfit.

But Anne should know, if not consciously, then unconsciously; for if Anne is her father's favorite and Rast Pronando's sweetheart, Tita is her rival. The small, ghostly half-breed sister is the locus for the virginal Diana's displaced feelings not only of violence, manipulation, and jealousy, but also of selfhood and passion. Père Michaux, Tita's confessor, is the first to identify Tita's "strong selfism" in her understanding of religious ideas: "Whatever was said to her in the way of correction she turned and adjusted to suit herself; her mental ingenuity was extraordinary" (74). Obedient Anne just "listened to the child with wonder" (74) as her sister revolts against the patriarchy of the Catholic Church.

But it is Rast, Anne's fiancé, who evokes the passion primary in Tita's nature and hidden in Anne's in a particularly telling scene, which occurs as Rast prepares to leave the island for college. As he bids farewell to Anne, she appears calm rather than sad, a reaction that annoys him. Tita, on the other hand, drops out of a tree into his arms. After giving her a kiss and stroking her hair, Rast is forced to pry her arms from him. Although Woolson is probably conscious only of how the scene prepares the way for Rast and Tita's marriage at the end, her language illuminates Tita's role as Anne's (and Woolson's) mad double crazed by passion:

> Tita, left alone, looked at her arms, reddened by the force with which she had resisted his efforts to unclasp them. They had been pressed so closely against the rough woollen cloth of his coat that the brown flesh showed the mark of the diagonal pattern.
>
> "It is a hurt," she said, passionately—"it is a hurt." Her eyes flashed, and she shook her small fist at the retreating figure. (120)

As Anne grows into selfhood, recognizing and acting on her own passions for Heathcote, Tita marries the colorless Rast, companion of her sister's youth, and then disappears from the scene. We learn of the marriage through a traditional women's writing strategy of concentric narratives.[30] Chapter 22 of *Anne* reproduces four different letters notifying the heroine of the events leading up to the marriage, which ironically frees her to act on her own passion.

Tita, whose real name is *Angélique* (like her mother's), is Anne's dark angel as well as nemesis. Diminutive Tita, full of strength of identity, is indeed, as William Douglas had noted, a product of some patriarchal sin. We read that sin as the father's denial of personhood for his daughters. Because of that sin, exemplified by his refusal to allow Anne to learn Greek, Tita rises to assert her own identity violently and passionately.

Despite their other differences, constituted in part by their differing gender viewpoints, Woolson and James are each concerned with the silencing of female figures. Tita, whose passionate nature presents a distinct threat to domesticity as constituted by the patriarchy, is silenced, and though Anne becomes an active asserter of selfhood at the end of the novel, in marrying she will be subjugating her own identity to her husband's.

Woolson's power, in *Anne* as well as in other fictions, derives from traditions of women's writing as well as from her own unique talent. The tradition is the most important element differentiating her from Henry James, a man who generally chose (the notable exception being George Eliot, a curious case given her choice of pseudonym) male writers as his models. We realize that Emerson spoke to him, not to women, like Woolson, when he wrote: "The Poet is representative. He stands among partial men for the complete man." One of Isabel Archer's mistakes is in thinking that Emerson wrote to her. Women, as Ellen Moers suggests by her recasting of Emerson in her headnote to Chapter 1 of *Literary Women,* are themselves forced to rewrite Emerson because they belong to a variant tradition.[31] Constance Fenimore Woolson found her representative poets in that tradition, in the works of Elizabeth Barrett Browning, George Sand, George Eliot, and the Brontës. Her individual talent is remarkable, too, not simply for her vivid local-color descriptions of Michigan, Ohio, North Carolina, Florida, and Europe (those landscapes which form the boundaries of her career) but also for her energetic struggle with issues of identity, language, and art.

Anne clearly exemplifies how Woolson adapted her literary inheritance from the domestics of earlier in the century to suit her original purposes. And indeed, her later novels take up that same women's tradition to tell stories of strong girls who triumph over obstacles to make their ways in the world. In her short fiction, however, Woolson treats issues other than marrying well. In fact, in several of her best fictions, marriage becomes the lesser of two evils, the other being destitution. Her artist-heroines are forced, in choosing it—and survival—to sacrifice self and art.

FOUR • "MISS ELISABETHA" AND "FELIPA": ARTISTRY IN THE DOMESTIC SPHERE

At the same time Woolson was working on *Anne,* however, she was also writing short fiction, a form she would come to favor. The stories of the *Anne* period, collected in a volume entitled *Rodman the Keeper: Southern Sketches,* include Woolson's first published narratives on the topic of artistry, a subgenre of women's fiction dating back to the early eighteenth century and the publication and popularity of Mme de Staël's *Corinne, or Italy* in 1807.[1] In both "Miss Elisabetha," originally appearing in *Appleton's Journal,* 13 March 1875, and "Felipa," published in the June 1876 number of *Lippincott's Magazine,* Woolson treats women's art of the domestic sphere as it conflicts with, on the one hand, the public art of the New Woman, and on the other hand, the subversive women's art born of the psychic "wild zone" of art, religion, and sexuality.[2]

Woolson's first artist-heroine stories differ considerably from the model created by Mme de Staël in *Corinne.* Whereas Woolson's heroines are confined to a private women's world, where domestic arts, such as basket weaving and landscape sketching, and the values they embody, household economy and realistic representation, bring tragedy, de Staël and her heroine Corinne are bold public figures. Eccentrically and gaudily dressed in colors and jewelry more appropriate for a twenty-year old, twisting a poplar twig between her fingers, thus suggesting a powerful and intimate relationship with nature, Mme de Staël was considered the first woman of genius.[3] Her heroine, given the pseudonym of Corinne, after the Greek lyric poet, does not carry the mark of the patriarch, a surname. Her real identity is never revealed, possibly to suggest that she is a potential Everywoman or to emphasize her marginality and final, ultimate voicelessness. She is a poet in the fullest sense of the word, for she makes worlds. Her male followers affirm: "Yes; we will follow in her track, and be such men as she is a woman; if, indeed men can like women make worlds in their own hearts."[4] Corinne is an *improvisatrice* in a world where "a woman was considered insane, or of doubtful virtue, if she ventured in any way to assert herself."[5] Yet Corinne refuses to hide her accomplishments, posing the rhetorical question "Ought not every woman, like every man, to follow the bent of her own talents?"[6]

Talented young girls everywhere read *Corinne* into tatters, identifying with her ambition, drive, and artistic vocation and thus giving birth to a Cult of Corinne.[7] One of the youthful adherents to the cult was Mme de Staël's countrywoman, George Sand, whose heroine Lélia, in the novel of the same title, dresses in men's clothes and ties back her hair. She claims to be Romeo, Hamlet, and Juliet, finally choosing the figure that best describes her: Corinne. What drives Lélia is her will to power over men: she is a woman with a poet's soul, an androgynous creature. She writes, "I identified myself with these images of eternal struggle between suffering and necessity, between rage and impotence."[8] Although her womanhood is reawakened in the power of nature, as a poet she is empty and powerless. As the genre developed in France, then, the female artist was seen, even by other female artists, as an exile, a freak of nature albeit an admirable one—in Lélia's admirer Sténio's terms, a devouring hydra[9]—driven into isolation by society as well as by her own expectations.

Across the Channel in England, too, the figure of the artist-heroine fired the imagination. Elizabeth Barrett Browning must have read both *Corinne* and *Lélia* before writing her own incredibly influential *Aurora Leigh.*[10] In the tradition begun by *Corinne,* Aurora's conflict of self centers on her dilemma of career choice: love or art. At every turn she must prove herself even before she attempts to write. She believes that men and women are equals, that women can spell, that just because she is a woman it does not follow that her writing necessarily lacks merit. In the end, however, art, though valued, is second to love. Love is, finally, of supreme importance in the affairs of men and women.

Across the ocean talented young women were recreated in Aurora Leigh's and Corinne's images using American characters and settings. The essential problem, how to reconcile their womanhood and their artistry, however, remained unchanged. Louisa May Alcott's little-known story "Diana and Persis" focuses on the friendship of two artists, one of whom marries. When Diana arrives to visit her old friend Percy, she tells Percy's husband: "But you know the wiseacres say we women cannot have all, and must decide between love and fame, so I am curious to see which of us will fare the best."[11] The message is the same as that of *Aurora Leigh;* the female artist can have one or the other, but love and art are mutually exclusive: "The same aim was theirs, success and happiness; but with Diana success came first, with Percy happiness; both being conscious at times of that secret warfare of thwarted instincts and imperious ambitions, the demands of temperament as well as of talent."[12]

The pattern of sacrificing art for love or vice versa continues later in the century with Elizabeth Stuart Phelps's *The Story of Avis.* Like Aurora Leigh, who leads a "sort of caged-bird life,"[13] Avis feels a kinship with birds, especially caged ones. Early in the novel, the heroine takes up a copy of *Aurora Leigh* in an apple orchard, a setting that suggests the incompatibility of art with women's lot as a result of the Fall: suffering pain in the bearing of children.[14] The scene implies, moreover, that knowledge of art causes woman's fall from innocence. Avis is "caught between two fires"; God has created two warring natures in her.[15] Like her mother before her, who gave up a promising acting career for her life as wife and mother, Avis is no longer able to pursue her art, to retreat to her studio, after her children are born. By the time her husband dies at the end of the novel, Avis's joints have aged, and her touch with the brush is gone. She must leave the fulfillment of her artistic dreams to her daughter, Wait. Like so many others, Avis, too, has sacrificed her art to family responsibilities and convention.

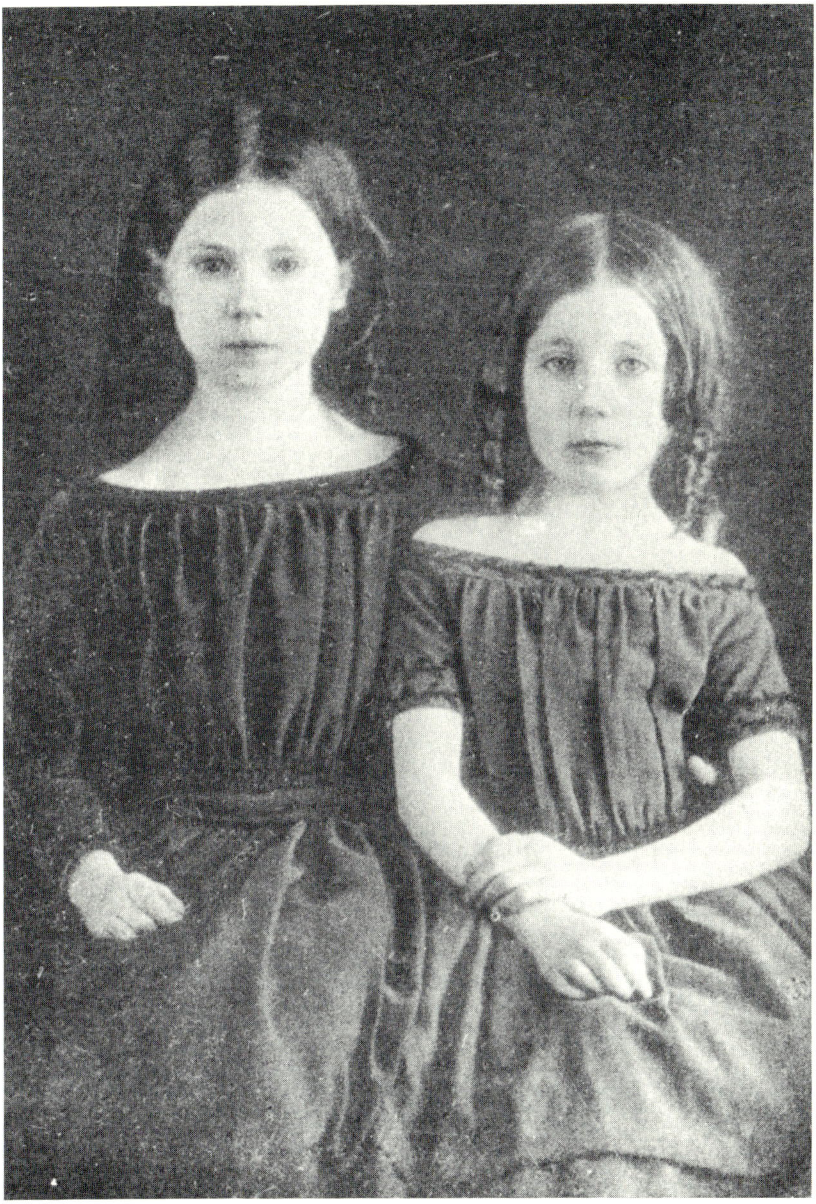

Constance Fenimore Woolson and her younger sister Clara Woolson Benedict remained close throughout their lives. (Photograph from ca. 1849, *Constance Fenimore Woolson,* ed. Clare Benedict)

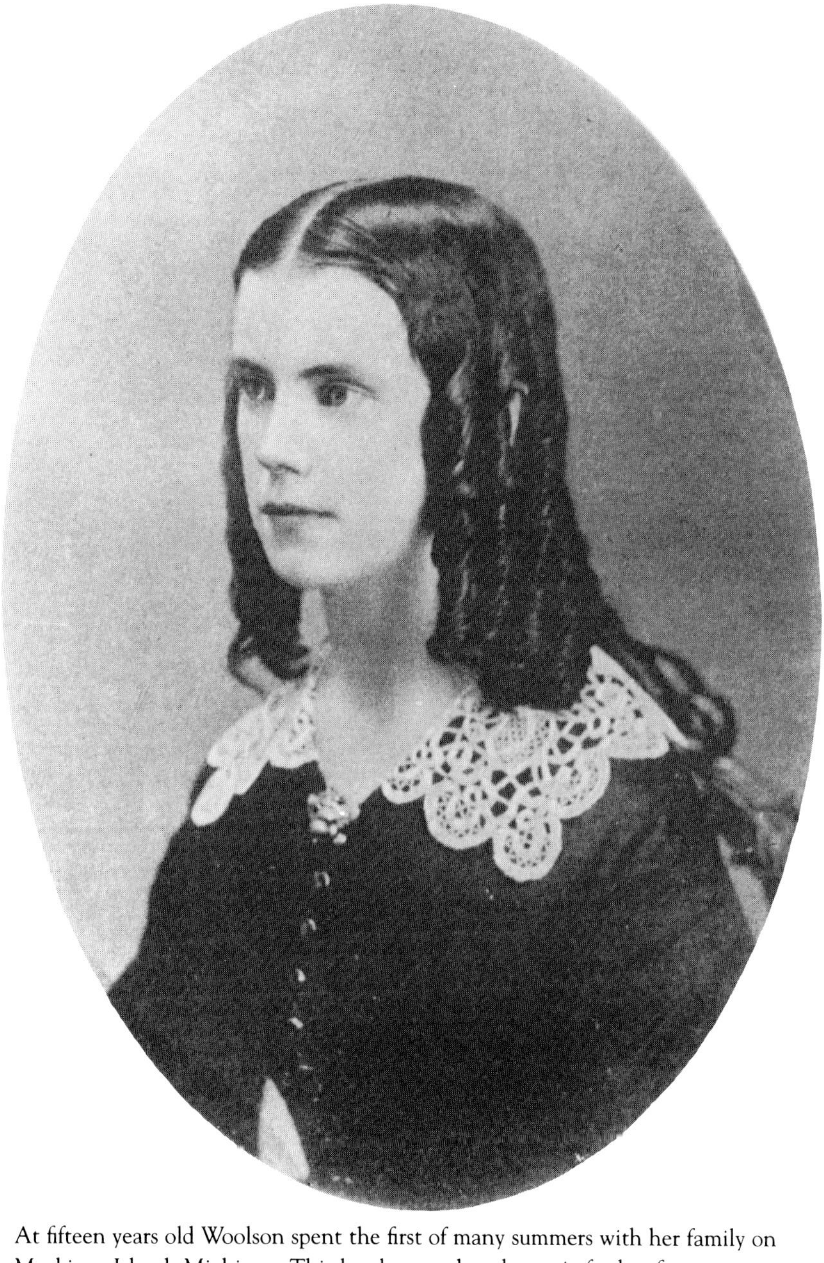

At fifteen years old Woolson spent the first of many summers with her family on Mackinac Island, Michigan. This locale served as the topic for her first two published travel sketches, "Fairy Island" (1870) and "Mackinac Island" (1873), and as the setting for her first novel, *Anne* (1882). (From *Constance Fenimore Woolson*)

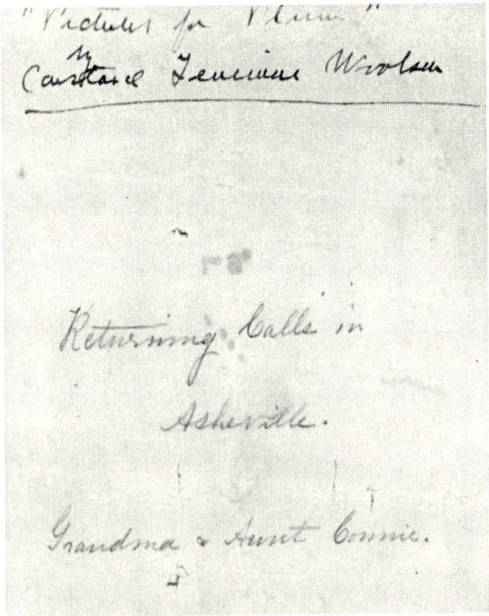

While visiting in Asheville, North Carolina, in 1874, Woolson sketched a short narrative to amuse her niece, Clare, who was nicknamed "Plum." Woolson casts herself as a determined, energetic, fearless young woman who braves wild animals and treacherous terrain to fulfill her social responsibilities. (Woolson Collection, Rollins College)

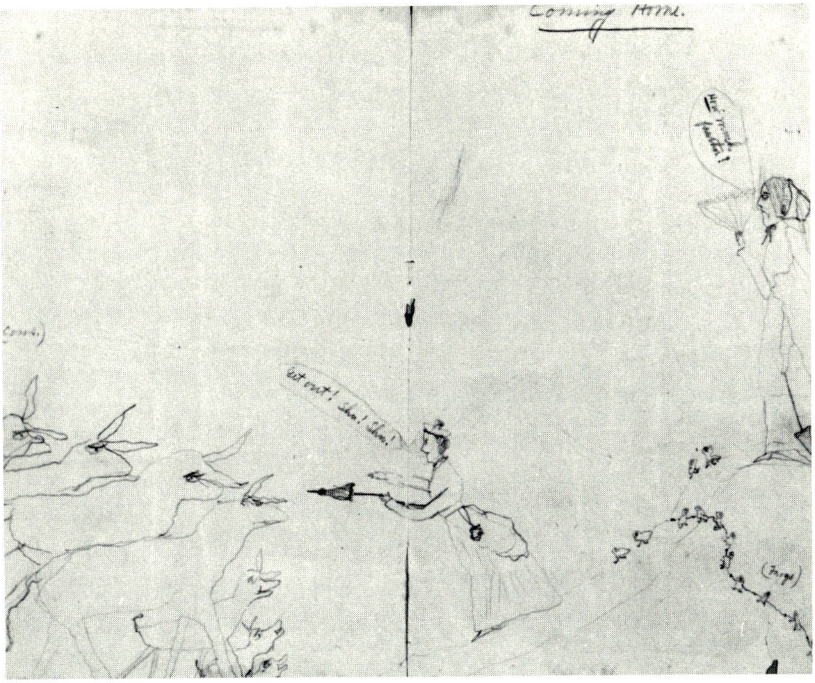

On the way to pay a visit to a member of the Asheville community, intrepid Aunt Connie fends off wild horned animals with the point of her parasol. (Woolson Collection, Rollins College)

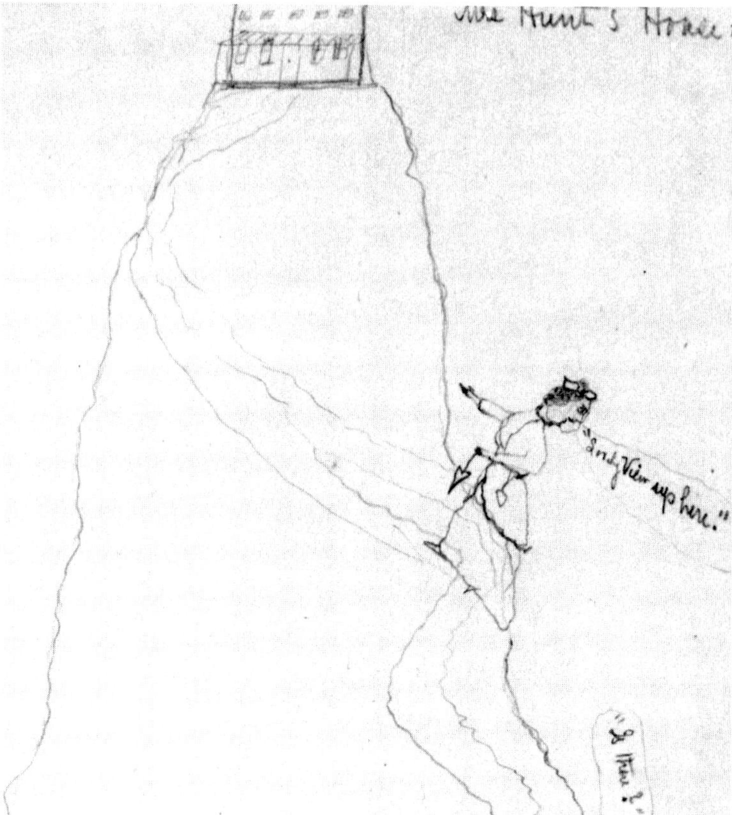

In "Mrs. Hunt's House," Aunt Connie encourages Grandma to continue the trek up to their destination, which is perched atop a steep mountain. (Woolson Collection, Rollins College)

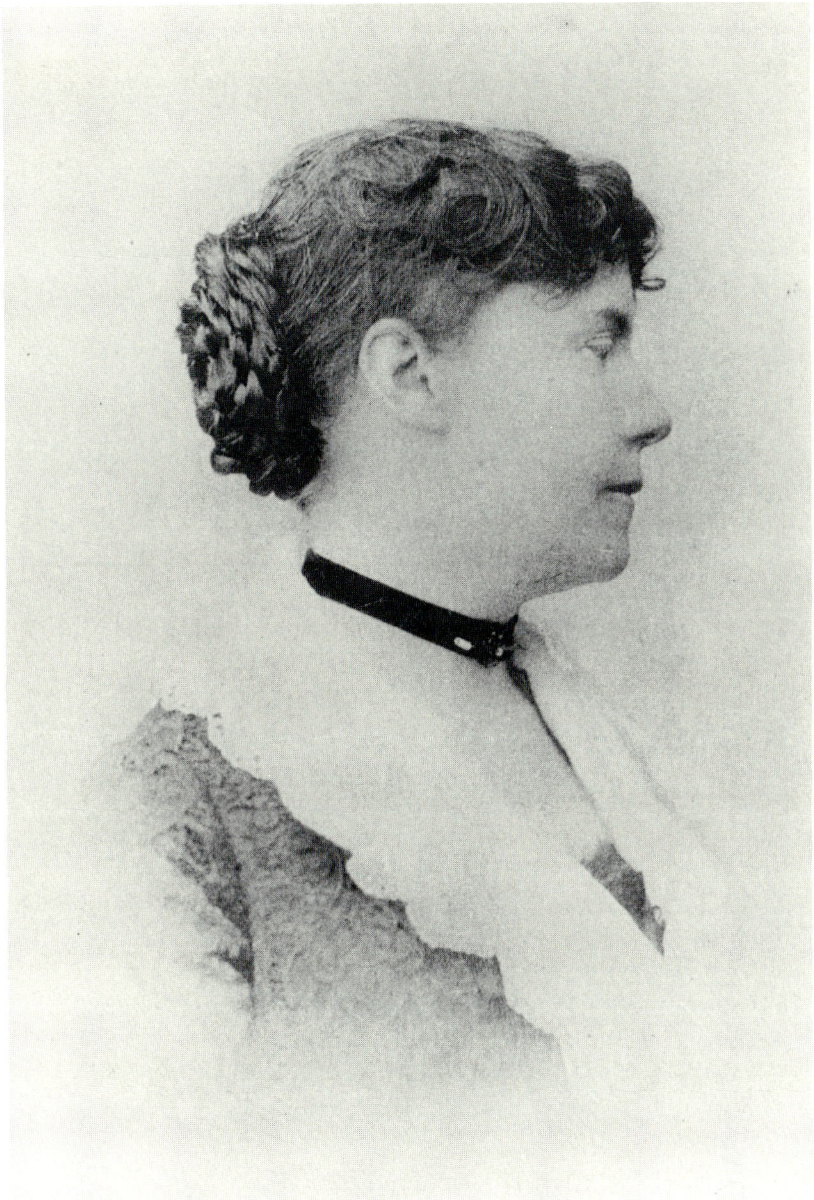

As a young woman Woolson devoted her life to her family and friends. Until her mother's death in 1879, Woolson wrote descriptive sketches, poetry, and some short fiction. After 1879, however, she went to Europe and focused on writing novels and her best short stories in addition to other shorter works. (From *Constance Fenimore Woolson*)

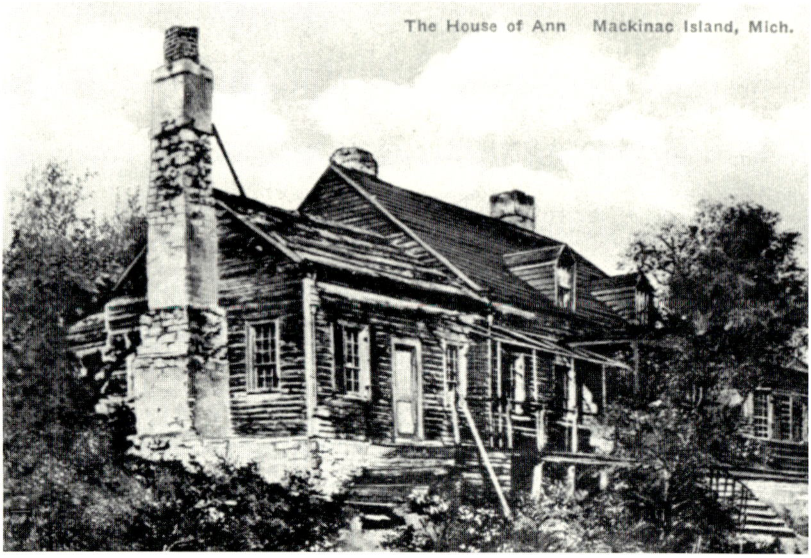

In Woolson's popular first novel, *Anne,* the heroine, Anne Douglas, lives at the Old Agency on Mackinac Island. The house on this postcard depicts (or suggests) the Old Agency. (Woolson Collection, Rollins College)

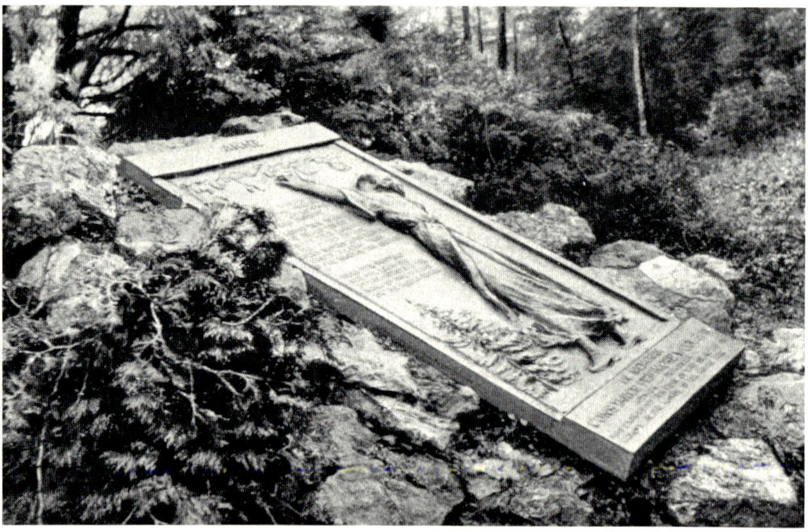

Like her heroine Anne, Woolson "loved the island and the island trees." A passage from *Anne* appears on the Woolson Memorial in "The Nook," Anne's favorite forest retreat on Mackinac Island. (Postcard in the Woolson Collection, Rollins College)

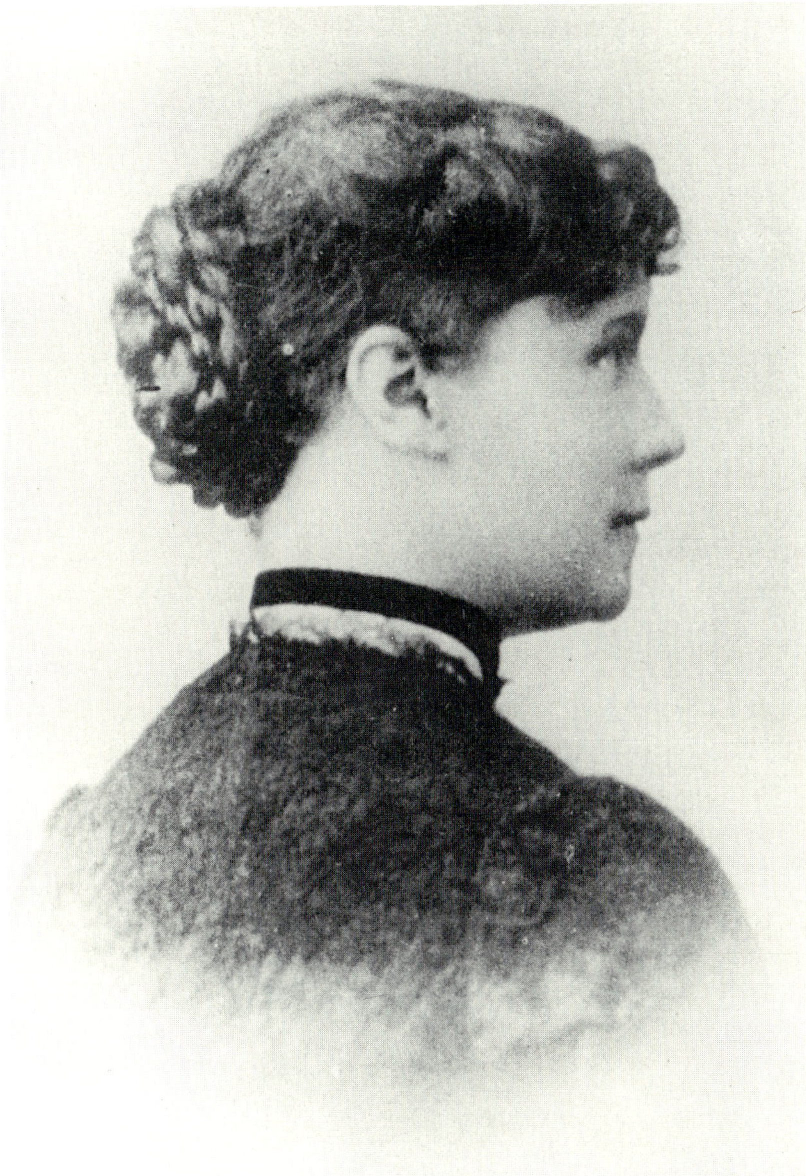

Woolson loved Venice, where she was able to live a quiet, economical life, and returned there in July 1893 from a two-year sojourn in England. "Venice," she wrote to her niece, Kate Mather, "is to me even more beautiful, more enchanting, than ever" (Mather Family Papers). (From *Constance Fenimore Woolson*)

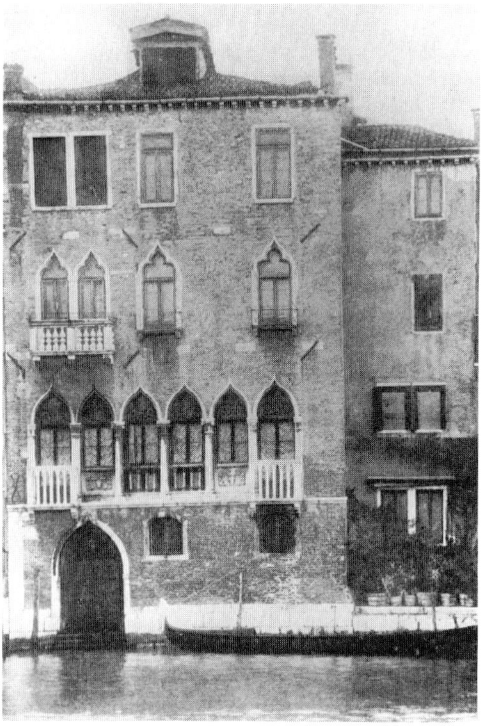

In autumn 1893 Woolson rented the Palazzo Semitecolo in Venice. Even Woolson's satisfaction with her physical situation, however, would not stay her growing depression, brought about by the onset of winter, growing deafness, worries about finances, genetic predisposition. In the early morning hours of January 24, 1894, Woolson fell from her second-story window and died soon after. (From *Constance Fenimore Woolson*)

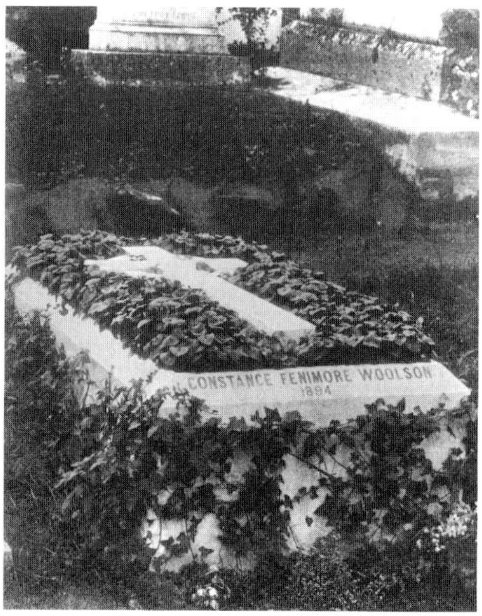

On January 31, 1894, Constance Fenimore Woolson was buried in the famous Protestant Cemetery in Rome. (From *Constance Fenimore Woolson*)

The earlier literary domestics had also written novels and stories featuring artist-heroines; however, their writers never perceived literary creation as a mode of struggle for authorial identity. The domestics' writer-heroines create as a lark or as a way to help with household expenses, as in Catharine Sedgwick's "Cacoethes Scribendi" or Fanny Fern's "A Practical Blue-Stocking."[16] Writing, for them, is never a way of asserting a woman's power of creation. For the serious writers, narratives of artistic development (or *Künstlerromanen*) are serious efforts indeed. They are assertions of creativity, equality, identity, and, perhaps most important, power. The women who write are women of might even though the patriarchal societies in which they reside—and the male literary tradition—deny it.

The tradition of the artist-heroine narrative was passed on, then, from generation to generation, from artist-mother to artist-daughter, in a pattern resembling the male *Künstlerroman* as elucidated by Maurice Beebe in *Ivory Towers and Sacred Founts,* but with important differences.[17] First, the protagonist in the woman's narrative of an artist's education is typically strong and sure, especially in physical terms; her male equivalent, weaker than the male stereotype, exhibits other traditionally female traits, such as passivity and sensitivity. Second, the female protagonist must choose between her sexuality and her profession, although her male counterpart does not face that crisis: he retains the ability to transcend the banalities of everyday existence, but for him the question is simply how—through sexuality or through art? Third, the female artist must contend with subversion in her own camp in the shape of the period's Total Woman: blond, lissome, lithe, demure, passive. Through contrast, this figure highlights the heroine's heroic capabilities. Fourth, artist-heroines do not idealize men or look to them as inspiration in the same way that artist-heroes make women into muses. Last, the female protagonist of the *Künstlerroman* necessarily indicts the entire patriarchy of her culture. She rebels against societal limitations while the male protagonist rebels against bourgeois expectations.[18] As Linda Huf puts it, "While the artist hero is only up against the banker and broker, the artist heroine is up against the wall."[19] Grace Stewart further explains the paradox posed by the concept of an artist-heroine: because we imagine the artist as one who is intelligent, confident, and self-motivated, "the procreative, other-directed, and nourishing role of woman is antithetical to the role of the artist. . . . one tradition of the male artist is experiential, a seeking of personal fulfillment; the other . . . is reflective, aloof, a self-centered and solitary existence. Neither tradition befits the womanly role of selfless involvement with and connection to others. Thus, the female writer must defy the cultural definition of artist or of woman if she is to remain artist and woman."[20] As a result of her peculiar catch-22 position in society, several images, themes, and patterns recur in artist-heroine narratives: "images of isolation . . . of entrapment, of flight, and of rebirth."[21] Writers of these stories demonstrate "a particular affinity for images of imprisoning glass—the bell jar, the bottle, the glass vase, or the spun-glass illusion"; the themes of suffocation and dancing; the pattern "of the labyrinth or maze, where the heroine faces dissolution or confronts her demon of destruction."[22]

Artist-heroine fiction, beginning with *Corinne, Lélia,* and *Aurora Leigh,* and continuing with their American counterparts in the fiction of many of the domestics, provided an important focus for Constance Fenimore Woolson, particularly after her mother's death. Early in her career, Woolson had produced fairly conventional love stories, in which the deserving young woman gets her man in the end, or in some instances, heroically denies herself a man's love because of mitigating circumstances. These fictions have as their themes devotion, duty, loyalty, sacrifice. After the death of Hannah Pomeroy Woolson in February 1879, however, her daughter began to produce tales of artist-heroines, who, though abiding for the most part by the limitations of gender in the tradition of the Cult of True Womanhood, at some point turn radical, much as Woolson herself did by leaving for Europe soon after her mother's death and neither taking up permanent residence there nor returning to America.

Around 1880 Woolson begins to use artist figures in her fiction for various ends: to represent women's marginality, women's creativity, women's identity. In many ways Woolson's heroines are the author's daughters, for her heroines play out her own precarious position as an artist on the edge of a changing world.

"Miss Elisabetha," Woolson's first story to cast an artist as a protagonist, dramatizes the clash between the private woman of the domestic sphere and the public woman of the heterosocial sphere. Because both women are artists, their conflict expands to embrace their art.[23] The story is this: Miss Elisabetha Daarg, a cultured, older gentlewoman, and her young ward, Theodore (Doro) Oesterand, live peaceful, ordered lives on the Atlantic coast of Florida, Doro singing, swimming, and studying, and Miss Elisabetha teaching, managing the household, and weaving palmetto baskets. Their utopian existence, however, is interrupted by the appearance of Cécile Kernadi, an opera diva, who, on hearing Doro's voice, wants to take him as a protégé and give him a European musical education. Beautiful as well as talented, she enchants Doro in what begins as a gender-inverted *Tempest* story. Miss Elisabetha, though, refuses to let Doro go. Realizing Doro's value for the old woman, Kernadi withdraws from the scene, sending an autographed picture of herself to the boy. Miss Elisabetha burns the image and begins saving her palmetto basket money to send Doro to Europe herself. Although he immediately mourns his lost love and opportunity, Doro, on reaching his majority, refuses his guardian's offer of travel, preferring to remain in Florida and marry a lively, uncultivated Minorcan girl. He marries, produces several children, and dies in middle age, leaving Miss Elisabetha to care for both his wife and his children.

Doro's dilemma is hardly remarkable except in its conventionality: the young, isolated romantic glimpses a lovely woman, unlike any he has ever seen, and falls desperately—and innocently—in love. When his love leaves, he cries, but he learns to love again. The real conflict is between the women who want to possess him, representatives of two opposing generations of women and producers of two opposing kinds of art.

Miss Elisabetha clearly belongs to a disappearing domestic world, as evidenced by Woolson's description of her person, environment, and attitudes. Her portrait is that of a fading belle, a woman bred to fashion, romance, and culture: values of the domestic sphere. Her hairstyle, for example, is dated, "adorned" as it is "with a high comb," a fashion long abandoned by the early 1870s (76). Moreover, throughout Woolson refers to the three thin curls of blond hair on each side of

Miss Elisabetha's face. These curls are significant not only because they too are passé but also because they suggest several characters in children's stories—from Goldilocks to the little girl who was alternately good and horrid—from the domestic sphere. From head to toe Miss Elisabetha perceives herself as a lady first, and her pride of class and sex extends literally all the way to her feet: "The ladies of the Daarg family always wore slippers—the heavy-sounding modern boot they considered a structure suitable only for persons of plebeian origin. A lady should not even step perceptibly; she should glide" (78). As she prepares to confront Cécile Kernadi, she is conscious that her dress encodes her values:

> The ladies of the Daarg family had not been wont to change their attire every passing fashion, and the robe she now drew forth was made in the style of full twenty-five years previous—a stiff drab brocade flowered in white, two narrow flounces around the bottom of the scant skirt, cut half low in the neck with a little bertha, the material wanting in the lower part standing out resplendent in the broad leg-of-mutton sleeves, stiffened with buckram. Never had the full daylight of Beata seen this precious robe, and Miss Elisabetha herself considered it for a moment with some misgivings as to its being too fine for such an occasion. But had not Doro spoken of "velvet" and "embroideries"? So, with solemnity, she arrayed herself, adding a certain Canton-crape scarf of a delicate salmon color, and a Leghorn bonnet with crown and cape, which loomed out beyond her face so that the three curls slanted forward over the full ruche to get outside, somewhat like blinders. . . . "Certainly I look the gentlewoman," she thought, with calm pride, "and this person, whoever she is, can not fail to at once recognize me as such." (91)

Her clothes embody a major value of the domestic sphere for women: protection. The clothes of the gentlewoman are her armor.

These clothes are only one manifestation of Miss Elisabetha's attachment to a vestigial domestic network and its preoccupations. Other examples are her ordering that an heirloom recipe for honeycakes be baked to coax Doro out of his depression following Kernadi's departure, and her covering the piano, which she tunes and dusts herself, with "a cover in cross-stitch, yellow tulips growing in straight rows out of a blue ground—an heirloom pattern brought from Holland" (76). Her domestic nurturing drives are exercised, then, against the vast field of Daarg women's history.

This history, as the heirloom piano cover suggests, is one of domestic artistry. Throughout Miss Elisabetha engages or is seen to have engaged in various forms of household art, all of which nurture, conserve, protect, fortify: she has knitted Doro's stockings, has made orange wine, and makes and sells baskets, historically one of the earliest artifacts of women's culture in many civilizations. These baskets are particularly important to Miss Elisabetha, for into their crafting she weaves her identity and makes a statement about who she is, a very original, self-sufficient lady in the old style:

> Miss Elisabetha had learned also to braid palmetto, and her long fingers, once accustomed to the work, accomplished as much in a week as Zanita Perez and both her apprentices accomplished in two; she brought to the task also original ideas, original at least in Beata, where the rude hats and baskets were facsimiles of those braided there two hundred years before by the Spanish women, who had learned the art from the Indians. Thus Miss Elisabetha's wares found ready sale at increased prices, little enough to Northern ideas—sixpence for a hat—one shilling for a basket; but all down the coast, and inland toward the great river, there was a demand for her work, and the lines hung in the garden were almost constantly covered with the drying palmetto. (81)

In the largest sense, Miss Elisabetha is an artist of huswifery, attending fastidiously to all the household accounts and regulating supplies of oranges, fish, and seafood. All of her arts, we note, are those of the domestic sphere. In fact, the several conventional emblems of male artistic inspiration—"a ruined fountain, a rose- and myrtle-bushes"—are located in an enclosed courtyard situated in the far rear of the house, along with two "ancient fig trees, dwarfed and gnarled" (79). Thus, Miss Elisabetha's male artistic ambition, as represented by her inner landscape, imprisoned and sublimated, is decaying. Her aesthetic space, civilized in its conventional symbolism, is enclosed and very private. In her sphere she cannot drink from the fountain, wear the myrtle, or offer the rose.

She may only engage in women's forms of the fine arts, and indeed, our first glimpse of Miss Elisabetha is at the piano, "playing, with clear, measured touch, an old-time minuet" (75). She plays, we are told, "in a prim, old-fashioned way, but yet well" (76), just as a cultured gentlewoman should; however, the music is rapidly fading (the E flat no longer sounds), and by the end of the story, the piano is broken by a new generation of "ignorant hands that sounded its chords at random" (104). Her music is the private domestic salon music of women's culture: the kind of music that Madame Ratignolle plays in Kate Chopin's *The Awakening*. Miss Elisabetha's favorite song is significantly "The Proud Ladye," spelled with appropriately outmoded orthography. Rendered in "prim melody," the song is a story of courtly love, one of the earliest forms of women's fiction. It is "the ballad of the knight, who, scorned by his lady-love, went to the wars with her veil bound on his heart; he dies on the field, but a dove bears back the veil to the Proud Ladye, who straightway falls 'a-weeping and a-weeping till she weeps her life away'" (76). Miss Elisabetha had been taught the tune by Monsieur Vocard, whom we suspect to be either a music master at the type of finishing school Woolson herself attended or a private tutor. In either case, he is a dictatorial figure of artistic patriarchy, who has led Miss Elisabetha to believe that artistic interpretations are patriarchally legislated. For when Doro slurs the vibrato of the old French *romanza* "into something like naturalness, or gave *staccato* as the mocking-bird throws out his shower of short, round notes" (77), Miss Elisabetha, in a learned patriarchal manner, reprimands him with her own example: "Taking the guitar from Theodore's hand, she executed all the flourishes slowly and precisely, making him follow her, note for note. Then he must sing it all over again while she beat the time . . ." (78).

Miss Elisabetha's domestic values and activities are thrown into relief when her antagonist, Cécile Kernadi, appears on the peninsula to recover from a cold. She is the New Woman, the antithesis of Miss Elisabetha in every way, as is neatly demonstrated in their first exchange. On being presented with Miss Elisabetha's card, the diva questions the name:

> "Daarg, madame," replied Miss Elisabetha. "If you have resided in New York at all, you are probably familiar with the name"; and majestically she smoothed down the folds of the salmon-colored scarf.

"I have resided in New York, and I am not familiar with the name," said the person, throwing her head back indolently among the cushions. (93)

Miss Elisabetha appeals to a knowledge of her place in a private family network, signified and made public by the name of the father. Throughout, Woolson's reference to the protagonist by the marker of her marital status and her first name, redundantly feminized by the addition of the feminine suffix *a* to an already gender-differentiated name, insists on her identification with the woman's sphere. On their first meeting, the diva is similarly incredulous when she finds that Miss Elisabetha has not heard of her; as the older woman had assumed knowledge of a domestic network, Cécile Kernadi had assumed public knowledge of her personal achievement.

In fact, what appalls and offends Miss Elisabetha more than anything else is that Kernadi is a woman who lacks a feminine domestic definition. She, a woman who introduces herself simply with "I am Kernadi," is abnormal by older standards. She is, the older woman declares, "a person of no name, of no antecedents, a *public* singer" (95, my emphasis). Kernadi's manner violates the boundaries of propriety as dictated by the women's cultural tradition:

> She wore a long, full robe of sea-green silk, opening over a mist of lace-trimmed skirts, beneath whose filmy borders peeped little feet incased in green-silk slippers, with heels of grotesque height; a cord and tassels confined the robe to her round waist; the hanging sleeves, open to the shoulders, revealed superb white arms; and the mass of golden hair was gathered loosely up behind, with a mere *soupçon* of a cap perched on top, a knot of green ribbon contrasting with the low-down golden ripples over the forehead. Miss Elisabetha surveyed the attitude and the attire with disfavor; in her young days no lady in health wore a wrapper, or lolled on sofas. But the person, who was the pet prima donna of the day, English, with a world-wide experience and glory, knew nothing of such traditions. (93)

Miss Elisabetha has educated Doro well to the music of the domestic sphere: the music of the drawing room or of the intimate musicale. But when he first meets Kernadi, she sings something that he cannot identify either by the language of the lyrics or by the rhythm and meter. He attempts to explain his fascination to his guardian: "Aunt, I can not tell you what it was like, but it seemed to tell me a new story of a new world" (85). From this description we can assume that Kernadi had sung an aria, perhaps in the high Italian style—a nondomestic song presented in public performance.

Both Miss Elisabetha and Kernadi want Doro for their own ends: the former for the private domestic purposes of preserving an earlier romantic attachment to his father and of maintaining her domestic culture fashioned around educating and financing Doro for the future; and Kernadi for the public purpose of turning him into a great opera singer and thus making him an extension of her own prestige and power. In other ways, too, these women are surprisingly alike, their differences being marked by their spheres of influence. Both women, for example, are types of Cecilia, the patron saint of music, often associated with women and domesticity. Doro pictures Miss Elisabetha as a St. Cecilia when her musical strains transport him to heaven. Kernadi's music also transports the unanalytical Doro to heaven; moreover, her name *is* Cécile although she does not identify herself as such, preferring the patronymic.

In their desire to get what they want, the two women are also associated with tigers. Miss Elisabetha is described as the female of the species in one of the most domestic of poses, as a "tigress defending her young" (98) in the enclosed area of Kernadi's drawing room. The diva, on the other hand, is presented atop a tiger skin (the beautiful pelt of the male), spread out on the beach in a public, expansive pose. Miss Elisabetha's art, dress, and imagery are derived from women's culture; Kernadi's are not. Both she and her art—high art, public art, art "truly the work of a composer gone mad" (89)—exist in territory perceived by Miss Elisabetha as foreign, threatening, dangerous.

The world of high art is not the only threat to Miss Elisabetha's easy domesticity. The other creative wild zone, that of sexuality, is the one that eventually lures Doro from her in the same way that, the story implies, it had lured his father from her. Catalina, a fourteen-year-old Minorcan, sings in a "velvet contralto, as full of rich tones as a peach is full of lusciousness" (100). Miss Elisabetha hears her voice one day and thinks it not bad, but deprecates that "there is a certain element of the *sauvage* in it. No lady, no person of culture, would permit herself to sing in that way" (100). Untamed sexuality, albeit sublimated into art, rather than high art itself, is finally the opponent against which women's culture cannot compete.

In "Miss Elisabetha" Constance Fenimore Woolson presents a parable of the generational conflict between the exemplary female of the Cult of True Womanhood in the person of Elisabetha Daarg and the representative of the threatening New Woman, Cécile Kernadi. Both women are characterized by their proper arts. The former, an amateur singer, pianist, and basket maker, is useful, domestic, devoted to form and decorum. Her art is akin to folk art in that while it is ornamental, it is primarily utilitarian. Elisabetha Daarg's is a private art designed to fulfill two functions: to assist with household expenses and to equip her ward with what she perceives as the necessary refinements of a cultured life. The latter is a public singer of opera, a high, artificial, and philosophical art, which serves no strictly practical purpose. Kernadi's stage is the world, represented by the broad beach on which Doro and the reader see her; Elisabetha's is the private, enclosed garden.

Constance Fenimore Woolson is neither Elisabetha nor Kernadi, nor does she prefer one to the other. She is, however, one of the first writers to dramatize, through the conflict between these two women, the problem of choosing between public and private worlds and to call into question the purpose of art. Her fundamental question is not which woman is the truer artist more deserving of the "prize"; it is, rather, given Elisabetha's and Kernadi's varying purposes, where does art lead? Despite her herculean efforts to protect and provide for Doro through her mastery of domestic arts, the changing world no longer values Miss Elisabetha's talents, and her art no longer protects her. And although Kernadi wishes to bring a new voice before her world of opera and culture, she too is frustrated. For both of these women, the single-minded pursuit of art without regard to sexuality leads to loneliness or regret; after all, neither artist, finally, gets the adored young boy, and both women are deserted in favor of an artless, natural native girl. Later in Woolson's career art will lead to silence, and finally, for at least one of her characters, Aaronna Moncrief—"Miss Grief"—and perhaps for Woolson herself, it will lead to death.

Like "Miss Elisabetha," "Felipa" is a *Tempest*-like allegory of art and sexuality set in the fictional settlement of Beata, Florida, but in this version the reader focuses more closely on the youthful seeker after both rather than on the struggle over the youth.[24] More precisely, in this story, Catherine, "an artist poor and painstaking" (199), tells of traveling south for her health in the company of her good friend Christine. There, on the edge of the great salt marsh, they meet Felipa, a strangely androgynous eleven-year-old, and her "second self," a huge dog named Drollo. The narrator paints her portrait, seeing beauty, courage, and love in the child's face, but her companion, Christine, sees only ugliness. The two friends become three with the arrival of Edward Bowne, Christine's suitor, and Felipa attempts to make them pay attention to her by dressing like a woman. Although Bowne and Christine agree that Felipa is greatly improved, they are in love and countenance only each other until a quarrel, after which Edward and Felipa romp in the woods. When the young Minorcan girl injures her foot, Christine becomes her primary nurse, rotating Felipa's care with Edward. Such an arrangement encourages Felipa to confuse the lovers. When they decide to marry, Felipa, in a fit of jealousy, eats the narrator's paints and allows herself to be bitten by a snake. Christine rejects the act of desperation, so Felipa attacks the object of her (Christine's) affections, Edward, with a dagger. All recover, however, and the narrator attributes the fit to preadolescent gender confusion although Felipa's grandfather disagrees, concluding "It was two loves, and the stronger thrust the knife" (220).

The specific geographical location of "Felipa" suggests the conflicts and provides an appropriate background for the story:

> It was a wild place where we were, yet not new or crude—the coast of Florida, that old-new land, with its deserted plantations, its skies of Paradise, and its broad wastes open to the changeless sunshine. The old house stood on the edge of the dry land, where the pine-barren ended and the salt-marsh began; in front curved the tide-water river that seemed ever trying to come up close to the barren and make its acquaintance, but could not quite succeed, since it must always turn and flee at a fixed hour. (198–199)

This geography very specifically raises issues of marginality, beauty, and male/female–principled relationships. The locale also lends a mythic quality to the story, reinforced by references to "Cinderella at the ball, leaving not a silver slipper behind" (199); the part-pagan, part-Catholic Minorcans; the ancient Greeks; Christine's medieval belt clasp; and the repetition of threes (three fellow sportsmen with Bowne, three other women whom Felipa has seen in her life, the three women of the story's love triangle). Moreover, the representation of these three women, Christine, Catherine (the narrator), and Felipa, within that landscape works toward explaining their complex relationship.

Christine's most revealing position is at her window. After a lovers' quarrel, the narrator comments: "If Christine had been looking from her window she might have thought he was not especially disconsolate over her absence; but she was not looking. She was never looking out of anything or for anybody. She was always serenely content where she was" (212–213). She is a Rapunzel figure, golden-haired, closeted, desirable, and, from a male perspective, completely powerless. She is the foil to the talented, self-sufficient Catherine. Although it can be argued that, insofar as she does not sew, Christine's domesticity is questionable, one can rejoin that she is created not in a specifically female image of women's culture, but in a patriarchal image of the beautiful woman, constructed, as she is, from the male conventions of feminine beauty:

> Christine was a tall, lissome maid, with an unusually long stretch of arm, long sloping shoulders, and a long fair throat; her straight hair fell to her knees when unbound, and its clear flaxen hue had not one shade of gold, as her clear gray eyes had not one shade of blue. Her small, straight, rose-leaf lips parted over small, dazzlingly white teeth, and the outline of her face in profile reminded you of an etching in its distinctness, although it was by no means perfect according to the rules of art. (198)

She internalizes these qualities and is thus unable to see in Catherine's portrait of Felipa anything but "an ugly little girl" (203). Her proper space, she perceives, is within the home as nurturing agent, so when she is able to step into the role of nurse after Felipa injures her foot, Christine radiates happiness.

While Christine is presented as happily immured inside caring for

Felipa, the narrator sketches at the salt marsh, that is, precisely on the margin where land, suggesting male-organized civilization and culture, meets sea, the primal feminine principle. The salt marsh provides an appropriate backdrop for one who is a locus of transition and transformation. Although Catherine, we assume, comes from a women's culture background, where gender roles are fixed, she seems none too sure of her own gender identification. She asks Felipa without apparent hesitation, "If you are a girl, why do you not mend your clothes?" When the girls asks whether she mends, Catherine's unqualified response is "Certainly: all women sew and mend" (198), as though Felipa has questioned her identity as a woman. Her response hints that she may be uneasy about her gender and that participation in such domestic activities defines and validates her womanhood for her.

Indeed, the whole situation—the setting at a liminal locale and the superficial manner in which Catherine conceives gender—implies Catherine's discomfort with her sexuality. Her closest relationship is with Christine, another woman, a "kind friend," who has been the agent in bringing the writer south for her cough. The introductory portrait of Christine, as "a tall, lissome maid," is a loving one, and, in fact, when Christine returns from the tryst signaling her engagement, the narrator admits: "I kissed her fondly—I never could help loving her then or now" (218). Catherine manages, however, to distance herself from Christine by internalizing male models of beauty as exemplified in the introductory sketch of her friend. Believing that life would be easier if her physical appearance resembled Christine's, sensing, albeit unconsciously, that if she were a Christine men would love her and her gender confusion would be resolved, Catherine says to herself half ironically: "Fate, in the next world make me one of those long, lithe, light-haired women, will you? I want to see how it feels" (216).

Catherine's vacation encounter with Felipa causes her not only to repress further her own sexuality but also to confront her patriarchal view of art, beauty, and religion. For the Minorcan child is a puzzle: her identity, unlike Christine's, defies conventional portraiture. Catherine describes her first encounter with the new standard of art, which defines beauty as the unusual, the strong, or the macabre, in other words, in fin de siècle terms: "I tried several times to paint Felipa during these first weeks, but those eyes of hers always evaded me. They were, as I have said before, yellow—that is, they were brown with yellow lights—and they stared at you with the most inflexible openness. The child had the full-curved, half-open mouth of the tropics, and a low Greek forehead. 'Why isn't she pretty?' I said" (201–202). Although the new definitions appear to her, Catherine cannot entirely relinquish her old ideas, her ties to tradition, so she seeks to discover the domestic vision of "latent beauty, courage, and a possible great gulf of love in that poor wild little face" (203) and to make the child over in that image. Felipa's appearance in new clothes, however, only calls a temporary halt to the war between what can be perceived as patriarchal and matriarchal philosophies of beauty.

Catherine's second experience with Felipa as a new model of art is even more significant. It occurs when, after the arrival of Edward Bowne, Felipa walks into the hammock chanting first his name and then the name of Miguel and his wife, two "apparently important personages on the canvas of her life" (205). It is in her vision of the wife of Miguel that her imagination comes alive to a powerful matriarchal philosophy of beauty, and new art is created:

> She lived on a sand-bar in the ocean not far from the mouth of our salt-marsh; she drove pelicans like ducks with a long switch, and she had a tame eagle; she had an old horse also, who dragged the driftwood across the sand on a sledge, and this old horse seemed like a giant horse always, outlined as he was against the flat bar and the sky. She went out at dawn, and she went out at sunset, but during the middle of the burning day she sat at home and polished sea-beans, for which she obtained untold sums; she was very tall, she was very yellow, and she had but one eye. (205)

This woman presents an image of harmony, confidence, and power. She and her art, polishing sea-beans—that is, creating something out of nothing, a woman's art, like quilting or basket making—exist in the imaginary wild zone inhabited by the muted culture figure, presented here as a transforming, shifting sandbar out in the ocean. Just as Christine, whose very name makes her a feminine adjunct to a patriarchal vision, presents an image of male-dictated art and beauty, this nameless woman out in the wild sets a radically new, seductive, subversive standard.

Felipa has the potential for existing in any of these women's worlds, and we see her in the spaces occupied by the other women in the story. For example, we see her in Christine's space, sitting in the doorway of the house. Importantly, however, Felipa is seated in the doorway, on the threshold, neither in nor out. She is a liminar, like Psyche, a heroinic paradigm.[25] We also see her acting, like the narrator, in the salt marsh, or rather, on the edge, where she lives alone with her grandparents. And like the wife of Miguel, she is pictured on the beach, "where she could gather shells and sea-beans, and chase the little ocean-birds that ran along close to the waves with that swift gliding motion of theirs, and where she could listen to the roar of the breakers" (202). She can also inhabit a man's world: as Miguel's companion she fishes and transports visitors with him. One of these visitors, Edward Bowne, even thinks she is a boy named Philip, dressed as she is in boy's clothing.

Her name signals her androgyny, and her androgyny suggests her potential both for sexuality and for art. Eleven years old, on the edge of puberty, she tries on both male and female roles as she switches clothing. Yet, even as she burns her boy's attire, she continues to identify with Drollo, her second self, a male dog. Others, too, think of her in masculine terms: Christine calls her a little monkey, and Edward notes her "muscles and nerves of steel" (207). Felipa, however, demonstrates no particular preference for either sex and settles on one or the other identity according to what she perceives as Christine's preference. Most upsetting to the company staying at Beata is Felipa's refusal or inability (this is hard to believe although it is the narrator's explanation) to differentiate between the sexes, suggesting that gender distinctions, irrelevant in nature, Felipa's world, are manufactured by society. For example, when Edward first describes her as "almost pretty," Felipa runs to Christine, announcing that *her* saying so has validated her beauty. The narrator remembers her own response: "'No, Felipa,' I interposed, 'the gentleman said it.' For the child had a curious habit of confounding the two identities which puzzled me then as now" (210). Later, too, Felipa cannot distinguish between the two lovers; when Catherine asks whether Felipa loves her friends, she responds:

"Ah, yes; it is so strong when they carry me," she replied. But it was Edward who carried her.

"He is very strong," I said.

"Yes; and their long soft hair, with the smell of roses in it too," said Felipa dreamily. But the hair was Christine's. (214)

Felipa's potential for androgynous sexuality, as opposed to the role-defined, gender-determined relationship like that between Christine and Edward, the group finds threatening, wild, and uncivilized. Catherine, especially, is disturbed enough to tell the story years after its occurrence; for Felipa is her mad double, as Tita is Anne Douglas's in Woolson's *Anne.* The prepubescent Minorcan girl acts out Catherine's own repressed sexuality and gender ambivalence, which surface in her retrospective narrative.

Felipa exhibits potential for the other important resource of creative energy: art. Unlike the narrator's art, which is dictated by patriarchal standards, Felipa's art is essentially female, and her artistic space is the wild zone, that primitive, metaphoric territory integrating body and nature and imbued with sexuality. We see Felipa, for example, "sometimes dancing alone out on the barren in a circle she had marked out with pine-cones, and once she confided to us that she talked to the trees" (201). Like the wife of Miguel, she lives and creates entirely in the wild. Felipa also produces a female art—creating artifacts from otherwise "useless" nature—outside patriarchal boundaries. Catherine recalls:

> Once we came upon her most secret lair in a dense thicket of thorn-myrtle and wild smilax—a little bower she had made, where was hidden a horrible-looking image formed of the rough pieces of saw-palmetto grubbed up by old Bartolo from his garden. She must have dragged these fragments thither one by one, and with infinite pains bound them together with her rude withes of strong marsh-grass, until at last she had formed a rough trunk with crooked arms and a sort of a head, the red hairy surface of the palmetto looking not unlike the skin of some beast, and making the creature all the more grotesque. This fetich was kept crowned with flowers. . . . (201)

Later Felipa rejects the doll modeled on the artistic—and sexual and religious—patriarchal values embodied by the male-identified narrator, who has given her "a respectable, orderly doll to take the place of the ungainly fetich out on the barren" (217). After taking the doll out of the house, Felipa walks to the end of the dock and casts it into the sea in an action reminiscent of the ritual primitive casting out of the scapegoat, thus purifying her world and insisting on its matriarchal values. The narrator is oblivious to the implications of Felipa's act, commenting only, "Well! . . . What next?" (217).

In the end Felipa rejects the patriarchal vision of both art and sexuality: two models that have frustrated her throughout. Her refusal to accept either is suggested by her suicide attempt through double means. First, she eats the narrator's paints, the medium of patriarchal art: an art inadequate to capture the particular color of her eyes. Second, she allows a snake, the traditional phallic symbol of male sexuality, to bite her. When Christine attributes the child's actions to a fit of jealousy, Felipa attacks Edward with Catherine's Venetian dagger. Interpretation of this final action is problematic. On the one hand, the androgynous child has internalized the artistic and sexual values of patriarchal culture by falling in love with Christine, and so Felipa's attack on Edward is exactly that of a jealous lover, as Bartolo suggests in the closing sentence. On the other hand, the stabbing is a tangible rejection of patriarchal art and sex, as represented by the only virile male in the story. In either case, the implications for the story are similar: the narrator, a male-identified woman artist, is caught in a transitional situation between a civilized patriarchal world of art and sexuality and another more natural world, where womanhood, art, and sexuality must be defined differently. Felipa, the androgyne—a symbol of artistic and sexual potential—brings Catherine to the point of conflict between the two worlds; however, Catherine represses her understanding of what has happened to her and the only thing for her to do is "to go away as quickly as possible and leave her [Felipa] to her kind" (220).

Constance Fenimore Woolson's first artist-heroine narratives, "Miss Elisabetha" and "Felipa," share a deep structure: both present young antagonists, Doro and Felipa, who cause the artist protagonists, Miss Elisabetha and Catherine, to call into question their very identities, and thus the efficacy of their art, the core of their personalities. An artist of the domestic sphere, Miss Elisabetha discovers that all of the orange wine, honey cake, and palmetto baskets in the world cannot protect her from the incursions of high art on the one hand and sexuality on the other. Similarly, Catherine is forced to confront her patriarchally legislated values as a result of her experience with Felipa. But Catherine represses her responses to the young girl's androgynous sexuality and wild zone religion and artistry in the same way that Miss Elisabetha refuses to understand why Doro chooses a Minorcan bride over the chance of travel in Europe. Both of these stories, too, are set in the identical emblematic locale on the Florida beach, where the shifting sand and natural rhythm of ebb and flow suggest the changing world Woolson and her artist-heroines, Miss Elisabetha and Catherine, inhabit.

Fewer than five years after the initial periodical publication of "Miss Elisabetha" and "Felipa," Hannah Pomeroy Woolson was dead and her daughter had moved to Europe, never to return to the Florida locale where she first considered the subject of women's artistry.

FIVE • "'MISS GRIEF'": THE GRIEF OF ARTISTRY

When it was finally released, Constance Fenimore Woolson's second volume of short stories, *Rodman the Keeper: Southern Sketches,* was met by excellent notices. Evidently, the politics of the publishing world had played a hand in the timing of its release, and Woolson had been helpless in the face of both her publishers' marketing decisions and the copyright laws. She had wanted to release her first novel, *Anne,* before the short story collection and then let the volume of collected narratives sell on the tide of the novel's popularity. But the publicity for both the novel and the short story collection was being jeopardized by the Osgoods, Woolson's publishers at the time. On 16 September 1877, she had written to her friend and literary adviser E. C. Stedman seeking help:

> I spoke of the Osgoods because it seems to me that they do not push their books enough. They merely announce them from their literary throne, and then sit down again. I do not precisely know what to do with "my novel," *when* it is finished (I have lost a whole year and more, owing to the depressed state of my mind, of which I spoke to you some time ago),—that may not happen for six months yet. Mr. Osgood will take it if I please. But I want to have it pushed a little. Hurd & Houghton offered to take the short stories the week after Osgood did. Osgood will bring out a volume of southern stories

(Rodman the Keeper et al.) this fall if I say so; but I do not think it will be any especial advantage to me; do you? It might come out *after* the novel. (Stedman Papers)

Woolson eventually withdrew her work from the Osgoods, in an attempt to solve her quandary. *Anne* was picked up by Harper's, and *Rodman the Keeper* by D. Appleton and Company, but even then she was unable to bring her hopes to fruition. Both the volume of southern sketches and the serialization of the novel appeared in 1880 though *Anne* was not published in book form until two years later.

Woolson's trials with the publication community regarding her volume of stories were not yet ended, however. The Appletons were a source of stress, as detailed in a letter dated 16 March 1883 to Clara Louise Stone Hay, the wife of Lincoln's former secretary of state, and popular author in his own right Col. John Hay:

"Rodman the Keeper" was brought out by the Appletons, on the terms that they should first pay themselves for the expence [sic], & then, on further sales (if there should be any), they were to pay me the usual ten per cent. They reported, at the end of the first year, that they had by no means paid themselves back, & were much out of pocket &c &c; a doleful tale. Last summer my sister wrote me that they had brought out another edition (a cheap one), on the tide of "Anne," I suppose. So not long ago I wrote to them, inquiring about this new edition &c &c. I never expected any *money* from the first edition—as that is not the Appleton's way! I wanted to have the book brought out at just that time, &, as my connection with Osgood had been broken, & the Appletons were urgently desirous to have it, I allowed them to publish it. My object now is—& has been for some time—to get it back into my own hands,—before making arrangements for English publication.—Well, I received recently the Appletons' reply. The first edition I *think*—1500 copies, in cloth—has been sold out. The new edition, cheaper, (about which they never consulted me) a thousand copies—is also sold—or almost. But they have still not paid themselves for their expenses, & have therefore nothing due me! As to the sale of the book to me—they *now* "do not wish to part with it"; they consider it "valuable." They intimate that if I insist upon buying it back, they shall feel obliged to charge a good deal for it; in justice, I suppose, to themselves! "Perhaps"—they continue—they may be able to begin paying me copyright next year. And then they close with a most earnest request for other books from my pen "on the same terms"! Is'nt that good?—I think I shall persist, & get the book back.[1]

The collection was finally acquired by the Harpers; however, as Woolson laments in a letter to Hay from Cheltenham, England, dated 20 December 1890, "By misunderstanding, the new edition (Harpers) was brought out just as it stood when recovered finally from the piratical Appletons. No one minds it but the author."[2]

This frustration with the recovery of her own work, in addition to other sentiments regarding the politics of publication and the politics of gender, surfaces in her next effort, a story that does not simply demarcate a line between "early" and "later" Woolson. In "'Miss Grief,'" the first story she published after her mother's death and her own removal abroad, Woolson finds a new voice, one full of resolve and power in the face of a still hopeless position vis-à-vis the patriarchal structure of society.[3]

To sum up briefly, "'Miss Grief,'" a first-person narrative from the perspective of a male literary celebrity, concerns a strange woman's repeated calls to his home. When, after the eighth call, he finally agrees to see her, she presents him with a manuscript, which he discovers is a remarkable drama. The narrator agrees to help "Miss Grief," whose real name is Aaronna Moncrief, despite the narrator's insistence on invalidating her identity and trivializing her ability by calling her "Grief." He assents to act as her agent in an effort to publish her play, "Armor," and several other works of poetry and prose. One of her prose pieces features a protagonist curiously like the narrator, who, blinded by his own self-importance, is challenged to be better than he is. The male literary establishment will accept none of the work, although one editor will consider publishing the prose piece on the condition that one character—a doctor, who is seen as a second Messiah—is excised. The narrator attempts this editorial task, but cannot complete it satisfactorily: "that apparently gentle 'doctor' would not out: he was so closely interwoven with every part of the tale that to take him out was like taking out one especial figure in a carpet: that is impossible unless you unravel the whole" (139). In the end,

Aaronna Moncrief dies, naming the narrator her executor and requesting that she be buried with her other manuscripts.

The story, though much remarked on, has often been dismissed. Woolson's earliest critic, John Dwight Kern, sums up the plot line as "essentially the martyrdom of an artist who refuses to compromise her principles for the sake of popular success."[4] Miss Grief's death, Kern states, prompts the narrator to devote "himself to high artistic ideals and to the production of the best work of which he is capable, regardless of popular acclaim or disdain."[5] Kern's reading, however, seems so much male wishful thinking since the tale offers no clear indication that the narrator is at all conscious of what has happened to him. More recently, Sharon Dean has cited the story as an influence on James, containing as it does, the metaphor of "the figure in a carpet."[6] For Dean, Aaronna Moncrief is art incarnate, and when the narrator denies her and what she represents—"the suffering of genius"—he accepts what is the only joy now available to him: the shallow quotidien happiness of the hearth represented by Isabel Abercrombie.[7] Predictably, Leon Edel uses "'Miss Grief'" to support his contention that Woolson had, like the title character, "a certain exalted notion of her own literary powers."[8]

All of Woolson's commentators save Edel agree, however, that the story is one of Woolson's greatest, but Rayburn S. Moore is the only one to voice the obvious question: Why is this fine story omitted from both of Woolson's next short story collections, *The Front Yard and Other Italian Stories* and *Dorothy and Other Italian Stories?*[9] The setting alone, Rome, would have qualified the narrative as an appropriate addition to either volume. Until recently, few readers without a large library at their disposal could read the story, available in the dusty bound copy of the *Lippincott's* May 1880 issue hidden away in the stacks, in a reprint of the story in *Stories by American Authors IV* (New York, 1884), in a difficult-to-decipher microfilm reprint of either, or in an academic collection of Woolson stories reprinted nearly twenty years ago. None of these was very accessible; thus, for most readers, the text, like the work of "Miss Grief" herself, has remained "unavailable" and unread.[10]

The implications of the tale go a long way to explaining why this story in particular fell into the crevice of time, or to use Aaronna Moncrief's word, the "void," even in Woolson's own generation. Since women's writing is often subversive, the reprinting of "'Miss Grief'" (and the publication of Aaronna Moncrief's manuscripts) would have challenged the reigning male values of the nineteenth-century publishing world. The absence of "'Miss Grief,'" however, elicits profound sadness for contemporary women readers interested in the fates of our literary foremothers just as her inability to publish her manuscripts causes Aaronna Moncrief herself intense sorrow. For although she need not choose between art and marriage, as many of Woolson's artist-heroines must, her creative desires are nonetheless stymied by men who, fearing her power and control, seek, perhaps unconsciously, to dismantle her texts, which are a metonymy of her self. In recovering Woolson's "'Miss Grief,'" we may resurrect the artistry of Constance Fenimore Woolson and of her alter ego, Aaronna Moncrief, recognizing why, until recently, the tale was forgotten, conceivably even censored.

One possible reason "'Miss Grief'" has not been readily available in decades past is that Woolson's fiction attempts to subvert male literary mythology, a proposal with implications for both political and social institutions. The goal of subversion and its ramifications are lost on the self-centered, love-struck literary lion who narrates the story. Declaring himself "good tempered, well-dressed, sufficiently provided with money, and amiably obedient to all the rules and requirements of 'society'" (123), the narrator is incapable of dealing with an uneven-tempered, poorly dressed, insufficiently provided-for woman who flouts the rules and requirements of his social milieu. Though more successful than she, he is forced to admit that the "authoress," whom he has designated "Miss Grief," has more power. An obvious representative of the ruling class, he strives to maintain his hegemony by controlling her work in the only way possible: by possessing and locking up the texts that potentially threaten his celebrity status.

In the same way that Woolson's text of "'Miss Grief'" may have intimidated the publishing world after its original publication, so do Aaronna Moncrief's texts somehow menace the narrator and potential publishers, for they offer the promise of a vast world open to women and present the Messiah-doctor, the creation of the woman writer, who will remedy her grief. Thus, "'Miss Grief'" becomes a paradigmatic story of nineteenth-century woman's artistry, a narrative that, given late twentieth-century hindsight, offers an ironic comment on the canonization of literary texts by implying that many powerful works by women were, in effect, suppressed by those male readers, editors, and publishers in positions of power.

The major issue in Woolson's story is, in fact, power: Aaronna Moncrief possesses artistic power, yet the narrator, whose prose is much less effective, controls access to the male-dominated world of publishing. Throughout the story he attempts to exercise his domination over her: by refusing to grant her access to him; by renaming her; by acting as her intermediary with publishers, though not in an entirely timely fashion; by forcing her to rely on him for sustenance; by taking control of her production. The pattern is reminiscent of the politicoeconomic structure of a slave state. (At one point, in fact, the narrator decides to call the downtrodden writer "Aunt," a title frequently given to slave retainers in the pre–Civil War and later South.) Thus, we can read "'Miss Grief'" as a script of classic class conflict. The lower classes have the potential for power, but the upper class can rob them of it because political convention is on its side. Since in this story the upper class is male and the underclass female, the dimension of gender becomes primary.[11] The underclass female has the potential for revolutionary power; the conservative male upper class recognizes this and manages to maintain its firm grip on institutions and conventions by rendering the underclass helpless.

This politicoeconomic pattern of unfriendly takeover surfaces in "'Miss Grief,'" a narrative that is much more than a tale of martyrdom for the sake of art. Because she is a writer, Miss Grief attempts to assert her power in the literary sphere, the publishing world serving as a metaphor for other patriarchal institutions, such as class. Aaronna Moncrief and her writing attempt to overturn completely male literary mythology, beginning with the religious traditions of the Old and New Testaments, and moving on to the secular traditions of the courtly and the domestic romances. In this way, Miss Grief asserts the potential power of her own artistry.

One of the first ways Woolson challenges the literary patriarchy is by subverting the religious tradition of the Old Testament. She gives her heroine the feminized name of the Israelites' high priest, Aaron, the spokesman for his brother, Moses. Although Aaronna Moncrief herself remarks that her own name, her very identity, had been altered to accommodate her father's expectation—"My name is Aaronna. . . . My father was much disappointed that I was not a boy, and gave me as nearly as possible the name he had prepared—Aaron" (134–135)—she nonetheless becomes the high priest of art, the voice of oppression, carrying out, despite her gender, the duties and responsibilities of the chief celebrant of the artistic faith.

The Aaron in the patriarchal Old Testament fiction is clothed according to God's order to Moses, set forth in Exodus:

> And thou shalt make holy garments for Aaron thy brother for glory and for beauty.
>
> And thou shalt speak unto all *that are* wise hearted, whom I have filled with the spirit of wisdom, that they may make Aaron's garments to consecrate him, that he may minister unto me in the priest's office.
>
> And these *are* the garments which they shall make; a breastplate, and an ephod, and a robe, and a broidered coat, a mitre, and a girdle: and they shall make holy garments for Aaron thy brother, and his sons, that he may minister unto me in the priest's office.
>
> And they shall take gold, and blue, and purple, and scarlet, and fine linen.
>
> And they shall make the ephod *of* gold, *of* blue, and *of* purple, *of* scarlet, and fine twined linen, with cunning work. (Exodus 28:2–6)

The descriptions of the various pieces of the costume continue:

> And thou shalt put in the breastplast of judgment the Urim and the Thummim; and they shall be upon Aaron's heart, when he goeth in before the LORD: and Aaron shall bear the judgment of the children of Israel upon his heart before the LORD continually.
>
> And thou shalt make the robe of the ephod all *of* blue.
>
> And there shall be an hole in the top of it, in the midst thereof: it shall have a binding of woven work round about the hole of it, as it were the hole of an habergeon, that it be not rent. (Exodus 28:30–32)[12]

In other words, Aaron, the high priest, is to act as an intermediary before God, bearing the judgment of his people on his heart. Moreover, his clothing, fitted like armor for a soldier of the Lord, especially his armorial breastplate and other adornments, are to be suited to his station, and his sons are to follow him in glory.

But Aaronna Moncrief, the high priest in Woolson's fiction, receives none of the consideration of her biblical namesake, for having already subverted her father's hopes for a son, she now threatens the literary patriarchy with her art. As a veiled woman with a shadowy past, hiding not only her name but also her residence, she appears a stock character from a Gothic romance, that very genre with its rapacious clergy and incestuous secrets undercutting the scriptural liturgy. Instead of being attired in splendid robes, she wears a rusty, damp black dress; instead of being honored, she is mistrusted and misjudged. Nevertheless, she retains a degree of authority. As Christina Rossetti, one of Woolson's favorite writers, wrote in *Seek and Find* (1879), "Yet has the Aaronic priesthood, no less recognisably than the other, both a real and a typical majesty of its own."[13] Aaronna Moncrief's majesty is indeed real in the way she adopts the role of the dying leader, surrounded by traditional religious offerings of "wine, fruit, flowers, and candles" (141). Her final words are ones of authentic majesty in the squalor of everyday life. She begs the narrator to help her kinswoman "to return home—to America" (142).

Through her given name, Aaronna Moncrief undercuts New Testament as well as Old Testament tradition. For the majesty accorded the Aaronic priesthood is, according to Rossetti, both real and typical, *typical* suggesting *typological.* Indeed, "one of the last representatives of the Aaronic priesthood" was John the Baptist, a forerunner of Christ, and thus a type of Savior and Messiah in his own right.[14] As another Aaron, then, Aaronna Moncrief is a type of Messiah, a harbinger of an artistic era yet to come, when powerful women will direct their own creative destinies, when the breastplate of the Aaronic priesthood becomes the breastplate on the title page of Moncrief's work "Armor." As a woman, she turns the New Testament tradition of the typological Messiah on its head, just as Florence Nightingale did when she asserted that the next Messiah will be female.[15]

The fulfillment of Aaronna's type appears in her prose piece as a second Messiah, "a physician of tender heart and exquisite mercy," who ironically "practiced murder as a fine art" (136). The answer to the promise of Aaronna's existence, he is, however, rejected by both the narrator and his editorial cohort. He is the mysterious figure in the carpet that the narrator cannot unravel and still retain the integrity of Miss Grief's fabric. Within the text as a fictional construct, he acts out Aaronna's repressed anger at the powerful publishing world: "by practicing murder as a fine art." Once published, the doctor can offer a remedy to Aaronna's *grief* over her artistic invisibility—her hurt, harm, injury, mental pain, distress, sorrow, that "keen or bitter feeling of regret for something lost" (OED). Unpublished, however, he is the promise that cannot be effaced from the tapestry of Miss Grief's text. Because he will complete the void that Aaronna, as a type, proffers, because the doctor as her creation threatens patriarchal control, the publishing world will have none of him.

Aaronna Moncrief undercuts the patriarchal New Testament narrative in yet another way, in her repetition and subversion of several of the Mary archetypes. As the mother who gives birth to her literary "children" in poverty, she imitates the traditional pattern; her children, especially the second Messiah-doctor, whose figure will not out, are full of power and potential, attended and praised by a wise man, a member of the patriarchy. They are buried with her, however, unread and unacknowledged.

Woolson's story also revises the Mary-Martha dichotomy revealed in the gospels of Luke and John. In Luke, Mary sits at the feet of Jesus while her sister, Martha, busies herself in the kitchen. When Martha complains to Jesus that although she needs her sister's assistance, Mary won't budge, Jesus tells Martha that Mary should be left to listen to the good word unencumbered by household duties (10:39–41). In John, Martha meets Jesus outside town and suggests his responsibility for her brother's, Lazarus's, death: "Lord, if thou hadst been here, my brother had not died" (11:21). Similarly, in Woolson's text the narrator, who sees himself as a godlike figure, is accused of having a hand in the imminent death of a family member, by an accuser who is, in fact, named Martha. Like her scriptural namesake, the Martha in

"'Miss Grief'" is a workhorse. She is also anything but serene. In denying the name assigned her by her niece, she confesses, "I'm no Serena" (140). Like the biblical Martha, she is also accusatory, but her anger will not receive the recompense of the miracle of resurrection. Not to be reconciled, she undercuts the narrator's text of self—the decent, rather good-looking, accomplished literary god—by suggesting his ungodlike qualities. Whereas Jesus declares himself the resurrection and life in the Sisters of Bethany narrative, in the Gospel According to St. John (11:24), the Martha of "'Miss Grief'" assigns the Jesus figure, who arrives to "heal" the dying artist and is charged with resurrecting her by publishing her "children," to the powers of darkness and death: "Vampires! you take her ideas and fatten on them, and leave her to starve" (140). Here Martha, long seen in patristic exegesis as the less devoted of the sisters of Bethany because she does not study the words of Jesus, is seen as the power to contend with. Her name, the feminine of the Aramaic *mar,* a lord, suggests her strength, as in the Provençal myth in which Martha holds up a cross, in the tradition of vampire vanquishers, to slay the dragon. The Jesus figure, the narrator, is revealed to be a powerless sham.

The subtle shifting between temporal and spatial dimensions implied by the title character's name and the archetypal patterns she recalls in her functions as precursor, promise, and parody lends a dreamy, otherworldly quality to the story, which subverts the narrator's attempt to tell a realistic Balzacian tale. Aaronna Moncrief's narrative voice, however, intrudes on his effort to present a comedy of manners. She recites hypnotically, her voice "clear, low, and very sweet" (126), his favorite scenes from his own work: "Her very voice changed, and took, though always sweetly, the different tones required, while no point of meaning, however small, no breath of delicate emphasis which I had meant, but which the dull types could not give, escaped an appreciative and full, almost overfull, recognition which startled me. For she had understood me—understood me almost better than I had understood myself. It seemed to me that while I had labored to interpret, partially, a psychological riddle, she, coming after, had comprehended its bearings better than I had, though confining herself strictly to my own words and emphasis" (127). We hear her voice again when she reads her own manuscript, "Armor": "All the strong passages were doubly strong when spoken, and the faults, which seemed nothing to her, were made by her earnestness to seem nothing to me, at least for that moment," the narrator confesses (133–134).

Just as her writing read aloud transcends the immediate reality of cold type on hard paper, Aaronna Moncrief's very style transcends the Balzacian realism the narrator claims to imitate, first with the drama, but more especially with the papers she brings along the second time the narrator receives her. As he writes, his attention is quickly fixed on the several manuscript books that she has brought: "Such a fantastic collection of words, lines, and epithets I had never before seen, or even in dreams imagined. In truth, they were like the work of dreams: they were *Kubla Khan,* only more so. Here and there was radiance like the flash of a diamond" (136). From the narrator's critical perspective, however, these works are all "marred by some fault or lack which seemed wilful perversity, like the work of an evil sprite" (136). This is not to say, of course, that her works are, in fact, flawed, but only that they violate the conventions sacred to the narrator: her use, for example, of the semicolon violates his grammatical expectations. His metaphor for her shortcomings is telling: "It was like a case of jeweller's wares set before you, with each ring unfinished, each bracelet too large or too small for its purpose, each breastpin without its fastening, each necklace purposely broken" (136). Purpose, however, should not be dictated by the jeweler but rather by the wearer. Perhaps if the bracelets and the rings did not fit, it is because the jeweler had either not measured accurately or had little idea of the dimensions of his newest customers. Or, to read the metaphor in another way, in Aaronna Moncrief's writing, each symbol of patriarchal power—ring, bracelet, pin, necklace—each token of patriarchal bondage, does not, will not, cannot hold.

Miss Grief, herself, subverts the narrator's critical expectations, which have developed in him as a reader of the patriarchal traditions of both Old and New Testament narratives, but also of the secular tradition, represented by the romance, both courtly and domestic. For example, the narrator casts his and Miss Grief's relationship in the tradition of courtly literature because, through using its conventions and inserting himself into the place of the hero, he can maintain control over her life and work. His own language insists on his mind-set. For example, he writes that he "should not have treated [his] visitor so *cavalierly*" (124, my emphasis), had he not been sure of her eccentricity, yet that she was "a woman—yes, a lady" (125). By assuming that she wants to sell him "probably old lace, something that belonged to Tullia or Lucrezia Borgia" (125), he implies, if not the courtly romance, then at least a later romance tradition, but for the same purpose of retaining power over the interview.[16] At last, when he agrees to read through her other manuscripts and she agrees to arrive at a time he appoints, he responds: "My chivalry was touched by this: after all, she was a woman" (134).

Yet the gender roles of courtly literature are reversed in " 'Miss Grief.' " It is, after all, Aaronna Moncrief who flatters and courts the narrator; she vies for his favor, not vice versa. While he frequently refers to his own weariness, she reads with strength, demanding that he consider her manuscripts, looking intently into his eyes. She is strong; he is weak. Finally, she, not he, is the soldier for art, the armored knight.

Other elements in the story suggest a role reversal and overturning of the contemporary domestic romance, a nineteenth-century form that featured a heroine's rather than a hero's script. The heroine's text is written by a beautiful young woman, bereft of family, who triumphs when left to her own resources. Her victory is celebrated with marriage; her reward is true love. Though apparently at the mercy of her reduced or compromised circumstances, in the happy ending she gets both what the reader had wanted for her and what she had wanted for herself: a loving husband. " 'Miss Grief,' " however, violates all of these conventions. The heroine is not pretty: she has large dark eyes and is forty-three years old though the narrator thinks her over fifty; she is "plain in feature, thin, dejected, and ill dressed" (131). Nor does the narrative end happily ever after: her manuscripts—her children—are buried alive. Miss Grief violates all of the narrator's expectations about the conventions of women and of women writers. Even from the first she flouts social conventions honored in society for their shoring up of the status quo by insistently calling at the narrator's residence despite his repeated absence. The narrator justifies his own behavior by reasoning that through her "persistent attacks" on his door, "she had sacrificed her womanly claims" (125) yet does not realize that those claims have been sacrificed to poverty, for, he is surprised to discover, she owns no small "scrap of finery" (135) to wear to their dinner.

Her drabness is contrasted with the golden sweetness and light of Isabel Abercrombie, the narrator's obsession, whom he describes with Gilbert Osmond–like proprietorship as a violet in a garden bed.[17] "And," he adds, "I liked her so" (139). When she reads two of Miss Grief's short poems, the male-identified woman, Isabel Abercrombie (a name whose rhythms and resonances remind us of the medieval romance), declares, "Her mind must have been disordered, poor thing!" (139). Like a man, she reads female assertion as hysteria. And when Miss Grief dies, the narrator vows never to let his wife see the drama "Armor": "For women will misunderstand each other" (143). He justifies his refusal to show the piece to Isabel by reasoning that he would be unable to bear the disdain her reading would elicit.

The narrator's effort to recreate Miss Grief in Isabel's image, the image of the heroine of the domestic romance, concludes the drama of her life. For he buries her along with her manuscripts, which are covered with violets, the same flower he has associated with Isabel. According to popular Victorian convention, various varieties of violets are symbolic of faithfulness, watchfulness, modesty, and rural happiness: these are all domestic, sensible qualities associated with sentimental heroines, with characters more like Isabel Abercrombie than like Aaronna Moncrief. Only through the writer's death can the narrator, contrary to his expectations, control her text of self. She will not be a domestic heroine, happy at last in death, like a straighter version of the Emmeline Grangerford parody. If anything, she is an Athena-Minerva figure, a warrior goddess, armed and armored with shield, spear, and helmet, who spins texts stronger than any man's. The violets the narrator supplies for the burial suggest his, not his wife's, fraudulent understanding of Miss Grief's work.

In life, Aaronna Moncrief's will threatens the narrator. She, for example, controls the issue of identity. First named Miss Grief, then

Miss Crief, she, in her own time, finally reveals her name to be *Moncrief.* The narrator attempts to rob her of her power of identity by preferring to call her "Miss Grief" even though he is informed by the second page of the narrative that "Grief" is inaccurate. His persistent joking about his ability to limit the visits of Grief on him hints at his character flaws and thus at his status as an unreliable narrator. In that unreliability, he is powerless to control either the narrative of "'Miss Grief'" or Miss Grief's narrative. That the butt of his flat jokes encompasses the potential for power in the story is suggested by the way her text subverts the patriarchal texts (and institutions) of sociopolitical, religious, and artistic life. Her project is to usurp the male power of origin. In other words, the source of the conflict in the text is the issue of gender, represented by the relationship between the narrator and Aaronna Moncrief.

Their relationship is gender-inverted. If anyone in the story represents the unflattering stereotype of the female psyche, it is the narrator. He is, for instance, vain, unable to see beyond a surface representation. His writing consists mostly of sketches, "interiors—exquisitely painted and delicately finished, but of small scope" (127). This evaluation clearly echoes the charges leveled against women writers, especially Jane Austen and the American local colorists, such as Woolson. He describes himself as "in a vixenish temper" (129), *vixen* in its various forms being a term typically applied to women.[18] Like a woman, he is guarded and protected by Simpson, his retainer, who drops the curtain, shutting the narrator up in the inner room, refusing to allow him to accompany his visitor to the door. Finally, the narrator's very sentence structure points to what many linguists would designate female gender-differentiated patterns.[19] Their research has determined that women tend to use more qualifiers than men, thus more words than men, to express similar ideas; women tend to use more tags and more interrupting expressions and to ask more questions; women subordinate more easily, a function, perhaps, of their political and social status over the centuries. Granted, these generalizations reinforce the stereotype that women are more verbal and less active than men, a stereotype overturned in "'Miss Grief.'"

The narrator's own writing subverts the image he wishes to project of himself as a member of the powerful literary patriarchy. To see that the narrator's language represents what linguists point to as the characteristic weak constructions in women's writing, we need only analyze the text of the opening paragraph.

> "A conceited fool" is a not uncommon expression. Now, I know that I am not a fool, but I also know that I am conceited. But, candidly, can it be helped if one happens to be young, well and strong, passably good looking, with some money that one has inherited and more that one has earned—in all, enough to make life comfortable—and if upon this foundation rests also the pleasant superstructure of a literary success? The success is deserved, I think: certainly it was not lightly gained. Yet even with this I fully appreciate its rarity. Thus, I find myself very well entertained in life: I have all I wish in the way of society, and a deep, though of course carefully concealed, satisfaction in my own little fame; which fame I foster by a gentle system of non-interference. I know that I am spoken of as "that quiet young fellow who writes those delightful little studies of society, you know"; and I live up to that definition. (123)

In this sample the narrator reveals several of his speech patterns, whose typicality is borne out by the rest of the story. From these structures, we may infer some aspects of his character. To begin, his use of the "not un-" pattern may suggest a deep-seated pessimism or inability to respond positively. If nothing else, the construction is wordy and suggests "feminine" indirection. The second sentence is a compound connected by the conjunction *but,* signaling a contradiction. The third sentence offers another contradiction, a question, and a conditional form, suggesting a lack of the sureness or firmness associated with male writing. Sentence four presents several qualifiers, while five offers what appears to be a logical conclusion preceded by the conjunctive adverb *thus.* The logic, however, lacks real substance. Throughout, the narrator's speech consists of those and other weak patterns evident, for example, in his rationalization for refusing to see Miss Grief: "But I should not have treated my visitor so cavalierly if I had not felt sure that she was eccentric and unconventional—qualities extremely tiresome in a woman no longer young or attractive. If she were not eccentric, she would not have persisted in coming to my door day after day in this silent way, without stating her errand" (124). The many negative inflections suggest an inability to express himself and, indeed, to think clearly. His very speech patterns indicate the narrator's own assessment of his situation to be accurate: "It was foggy without, and very foggy within" (129).

Aaronna Moncrief's writing and speech are far different. Her poems, for example, "were simply unrestrained, large, vast, like the skies or the wind" (139). Her writing, resembling Walt Whitman's more than Jane Austen's, suggests her firm sense of self, a sense validated by her refusal to permit her texts to be altered by editors until the question becomes purely economic. The typical mood of her sentences—indicative, beginning with the subject rather than with a subordinate, frequently conditional, clause—further insists on her firmness of purpose. Many of her sentences point to issues of will, yet she does not seem to possess a conditional frame of mind. For example, she asserts, "I will not read it, but recite it" (133), when introducing the narrator to her work, and "I will come" (135), when he asks her to dinner. As he tells her, "Miss Crief, your drama seems to me full of original power" (131).

Herein lies the danger for the literary patriarchy, the reason, perhaps, that Woolson's story has rarely been reprinted: Miss Grief possesses original power.

As recent poststructuralist criticism has shown, the notion of origin is a patriarchal concept central to Western thought. The father-author as originator of text develops from logocentric philosophy, which has it that in the beginning there was the Power of the Word, God-given, in one form, to Adam. In his capacity as namer, Adam became, like God, an author. That authorship was never deemed an appropriate power for women is first made evident in the Old Testament creation myth, where Eve's ambition leads to disaster. In Woolson's day women writers' ambition continued to be criticized and was offered as a cause for illness and marital discord. Scorned as ugly bluestockings who could not get a man if they tried, women writers were demeaned by being called "scribblers" and "authoresses," as the narrator calls Miss Grief. Ursula LeGuin recognizes the tradition of denying or criticizing women's right to name in the recent story "She Unnames Them."[20]

Her Eve, in a subversive move to protest the limits of her linguistic power to name, asserts her power of gender by removing the names Adam has assigned to the Edenic plants and animals.

Miss Grief, however, has seized the authorial power of light, of the origin itself, as implied by the glowing terms in which the narrator speaks of her and her work. She possesses, he tells us, the "divine spark of genius," and her drama contains "scattered rays of splendor" (131). For this reason, the narrator feels as though, like God the original author, who created man in his own image, she is deserving of worship. He confesses: "I felt as if I ought to go down on my knees before her, and entreat her to take her proper place of supremacy at once" (131). She is a usurper, however; she must first be armored to take her rightful place.

In 1880 this difference was threatening. Those in power, in the case of Aaronna Moncrief, the narrator, who is a writer, and his cohorts, the editorial establishment, were not about to admit women to their ranks. Many undoubtedly shared the perspective of Aunt Martha, who compares the members of the male literary establishment to vampires (140).[21] The "authoresses" could, of course, scribble, but they could not control, as a sentimental engraving from *Harper's Monthly Magazine* entitled "Alden saying 'no' to a lady author" so clearly brings home.[22] These writers were like Woolson. Sensing themselves on the cutting edge of something big, full of potential, they nonetheless knew that fulfillment would occur at a later date. Their armor, a symbol of strength, is also a sign of their invisibility, for it covers the body. For Woolson, a fluent speaker of French, the story of Aaronna Moncrief is *her* grief, for it will remain, for some time, "unlearned," because the male establishment neglects to ask the proper questions about her history. The subversive subtext of "Miss Grief" insists on the woman artist's potential for power. In Woolson's day, however, that promise was not to be realized. For writers like Aaronna Moncrief and Constance Fenimore Woolson, artistry would bring grief, rather than triumph.

SIX • REWRITING MADAME DE STAËL: WOOLSON'S "AT THE CHÂTEAU OF CORINNE"

The theme of the impossibility of a woman's living a happy life of creative artistry remained a constant in Woolson's fiction beginning with her move to Europe and "'Miss Grief.'" One of the next stories she would undertake expands the theme intertextually, implicating women's artistry across time, through the eighteenth and early nineteenth centuries, and even across intellectual space, into myth and the realms of the subconscious. For the longer Woolson lived in Europe, a continent where the margins of time are blurred, the more she came to examine the universality of the conflict between a woman's artistic vocation and the life that society dictates she live.

During the summer and fall following the publication of "'Miss Grief,'" Woolson lived in Geneva. A letter to her niece Katherine L. Mather dated 2 October 1880 details her activities in that cradle of literary activity:

> I am going to Coppet soon, to see the house of Madame de Staël, or rather, to stand there just for its association with her and Madame Récamier. And to "Ferney" where Voltaire lived. I have found a delightful French library here, and am deep in the literature of Lac Leman; not only all the poetry, philoso-

phy, etc., but any number of the books of those French women of the 18th. century, who wrote such voluminous "Memoirs." (Mather Family Papers)

Obviously fascinated, Woolson reads unceasingly until, she writes her nephew, "I feel as if I had been the intimate friend of Mesdames Récamier and de Staël."[1] Undoubtedly, Woolson had first read the works of eighteenth-century French writers as a schoolgirl at Madame Chegaray's French academy; now, however, she was reading them again, and the narratives of women of genius would have struck her with added impact.

Rereading these works and visiting Mme de Staël's home in exile may have proved a déjà-vu for the American writer, for soon after her visit, she wrote "At the Château of Corinne," a long story of female artistry in the tradition of artist-heroine fiction, an intertextual construct in which she, Constance Woolson, writes of Katharine just as Mme de Staël wrote of Corinne; and just as Mme de Staël became Corinne in the eyes of the public, so Constance Woolson becomes if not the physical twin of Katharine Winthrop, then at least her alliterative double.[2] Melting and merging into each other on the banks of Lac Leman, Woolson/Katharine and Mme de Staël/Corinne all take part in the tragedy of the woman artist's fate as Woolson perceived it: silence.

The Corinne of the title is, of course, the brilliant Mme de Staël, whose novel *Corinne, or Italy* (1807), became the holy text of a cult, "*the* book of the woman of genius," as Ellen Moers points out.[3] Consumed voraciously by a century of exceptional young women, such as Elizabeth Barrett, George Sand, George Eliot, the Brontës, Harriet Beecher, Margaret Fuller, Kate Chopin, and Sarah Orne Jewett, *Corinne* stars an incredibly intelligent and independently wealthy *improvisatrice,* who falls in love with a man hardly her equal either in strength of character or in intellect, a young English nobleman named Nelvil. She introduces him to the artistic wonders of Italy, but he eventually leaves her to her art, only to meet and marry her golden-haired half sister, Lucy.

One of the keystones of the women's *Künstlerroman* tradition, *Corinne, or Italy* focuses on what for a nineteenth-century writer was not a false dilemma: private or public life, personal happiness or art. Even the title insists on the choice that the female artist must make: Corinne (the proper, personal name, the private life) *or* Italy (the public, the artistic world). The choice, however, is not the woman artist's but rather that of a society that dictates that fame and love are for women opposing, mutually exclusive forces. In *Corinne,* the heroine is destroyed "by a distorting social order, where all women must tend to a single ideal, measure themselves against it, 'understand' themselves through its reflection of their nature, denying any other."[4] This social order in which True Womanhood is prized above the individual talent drives women of genius mad. Madelyn Gutwirth explains the dynamic of this societal convention:

> The madness with which Corinne is threatened is a terror of invisibility. In all the scenes of despair in Mme de Staël's work, it is nonrecognition of the heroine *as herself* by the beloved, and through him by the world, that is the cause of the trauma. It is the ultimate lack of seriousness in the quality of attention that is accorded woman by man and by society that calls up this fear of nothingness, cause of so much genuine, nonfictional madness in women.[5]

Although *Corinne* ends with the death of the heroine, the reader is given small solace in knowing that the artist's genius will live on because she had been tutoring the daughter of her half sister and her former lover.

That Corinne's fear and Katharine Winthrop's terrors emanate not from their own souls but rather from an institutionalized patriarchal system they cannot fight is easily granted, even with no other evidence than a general knowledge of social history. Yet, the three instances on which a modern critic has commented on "At the Château of Corinne" have yielded not a single reading that takes the women's tradition of the *Künstlerroman* into account. John Dwight Kern thinks the characters "little more than stock figures in the author's repertory of romance," and though Arthur Hobson Quinn is approving, noting that Woolson "puts the case for her own manner brilliantly" in the story, he is hardly precise.[6] Rayburn S. Moore offers the most detailed exposition of the narrative:

> Miss Woolson has certainly told better stories, but nowhere does she make a more earnest effort to point out the inadequacy of the sentimental approach to literature. John Ford tells Katharine Winthrop that "women do not believe in truth for its own sake; it strikes them as crude." No American writer in the late nineteenth century respected the truth more than Constance Woolson, but one infers from this story and others that she was not always able to overcome the frailties of her sex and that, on occasion, the truth did appear to be too "crude" for literature as she viewed it.[7]

All of these men have missed the point, however. In neglecting to analyze the narrative in the context of women's writing, they have failed to recognize the connections among Mme de Staël/Corinne, Katharine Winthrop, and Constance Woolson. They have read "At the Château of Corinne" as a traditional heroine's romance in which the clever protagonist lunges and parries with her male antagonist until he proposes marriage. They marry, and, as the structural thread of the story knots itself up, they live happily ever after. A close reading of the narrative reveals, however, that the story ends tragically, with the heroine's isolation and artistic death. "At the Château of Corinne," for all of its connections with the history of women's writing, seems to be a reflection on the business of women's artistry and on the history of women as readers and writers, rather than a happy romance. It is a narrative account of the fall of women's writing into the abyss after the demise of the Cult of True Womanhood and before the advent of the New Woman; it is also, more broadly, the tragic story of how all women in all ages, the woman of genius serving as representative for all of her sisters, are appropriated, their subversive voices silenced, by the patriarchy.

The story is this.[8] Katharine Winthrop, a young American widow, lives peacefully in a villa on the shore of Lac Leman (Lake Geneva) with her cousins Sylvia (an older woman) and H. Walpole, until Sylvia's nephew John Ford arrives for a visit and instantly becomes Mrs. Winthrop's antagonist. Although he refuses to stay at the villa, Ford drops in for daily visits. One day Katharine's suitor, a poet with the appropriately romantic name of Lorimer Percival, stops by as he has evidently done at other times earlier in the season, and the group decides to make a "pilgrimage-picnic" to Coppet, the home of the exiled Mme de Staël. There they are received by the caretaker, Benjamin Franklin, who permits them to wander through the home and grounds. The group's conversation is devoted to the habits and exploits of Mme de Staël and her friend Mme Récamier. At one point Mrs. Winthrop asks each of the men which of the two women he would have preferred. Percival and Walpole name Mme de Staël, but Ford comments, "Between the two, there would hardly have been one" (256). Although Sylvia tries to smooth over his implied rejection of Katharine's heroine, this remark is the first indication that Ford cares not a whit for woman's genius. Percival then offers an elaborate toast to these female geniuses, suggesting that the reason the works of these talented women have become mute is that modern criticism is inadequate to judge them: "Was it all declamation merely, because, weighed in our severer balances, your lives were not always in accordance with it? Are there not other balances?" (258).

Percival departs soon after the visit, leaving Ford to the group of Americans. One afternoon Ford and Mrs. Winthrop stop at Coppet during a horseback ride through the area. There the discussion disintegrates from witty repartee to outright argument, ending in Ford's departure for Italy. The disagreement had begun with differing assessments of Mme de Staël: Ford had declared her an egotist, but when Katharine rejoins that she was nonetheless a woman of genius, the argument breaks open:

> "A woman of genius! And what is the very term but a stigma? No woman is so proclaimed by the great brazen tongue of the Public unless she has thrown away her birthright of womanly seclusion for the miserable mess of pottage called 'fame.'"
>
> "The seclusion of a convent? or a prison?"
>
> "Neither. Of a home." (263)

This disagreement becomes more personal when Ford declares his pity for literary women before knowing that Mrs. Winthrop publishes poetry, albeit anonymously. His response is "Better anonymously than avowedly" (264). She does, however, convince him to offer an opinion of a volume of her poetry, with which he is already familiar, and she is surprised by his criticism:

> "The poem, which you now tell me is yours, had, as its distinguishing feature, a certain daring. Regarding its other points: its rhythm was crude and unmelodious; its coloring was exaggerated—reading it, one was cloyed with color; its logic—for there was an attempt at logic—was utterly weak." (267)

It is not so much his criticism of her poetry, however, that shocks Katharine as it is his following explanation:

> "We do not expect great poems from women any more than we expect great pictures; we do not expect strong logic any more than we expect brawny muscle. A woman's poetry is subjective. But what cannot be forgiven—at least in my opinion—is that which I have called the distinguishing feature of the volume, a certain sort of daring. This is its essential, unpardonable sin. Not because it is in itself dangerous; it has not force enough for that; but because it comes, and can be recognized at once as coming, from the lips of a woman. For a woman should not dare in that way. Thinking to soar, she invariably descends. Her mental realm is not the same as that of man; lower, on the same level, or far above, it is at least different. And to see her leave it, and come in all her white purity, which must inevitably be soiled, to the garish arena where men are contending, where the dust is rising, and the air is tainted and heavy—this is indeed a painful sight. Every honest man feels like going to her, poor mistaken sibyl that she is, closing her lips with gentle hand, and leading her away to some far spot among the quiet fields, where she can learn her error and begin her life anew. To the pity of it is added the certain truth that if the words she sang could be carried out to their logical end, if they were to be clothed in the hard realities of life and set up before her, they would strike first the poor creature who was chanting them, and crush her to the dust." (268)

After some short exchanges, Ford attempts to make up to her by asking that she take his comments like a True Woman, in the spirit in which they were made, in other words, to respond obediently as she would to a master: "Show me the sweet side of your nature, the gentle, womanly side, and I will then be your suitor indeed" (269). If she behaves as prescribed by patriarchal society—like a True Woman—the master will consider acquiring her for his household.

The following summer Ford returns to visit his aunt at the villa, and another scene transpires at Coppet, this on the subject of Percival's marriage to a seventeen-year-old girl. Katharine and Ford meet yet a fifth time, that fall at the château after Ford has been summoned to the villa by his aunt. Depressed, Katharine has been riding in the rain when Ford approaches and declares his love, confessing that he has returned out of pity, having discovered that she has lost her fortune. He explains:

> "I am sorry on your account that your fortune is gone, or nearly gone; but on my own, how can I help being glad? It was a barrier between us, which, as I am, and as you are—but principally as you are—would have been, I fear, a hopeless one. I doubt if I should ever have surmounted it. Your loss brings you nearer to me—the woman I deeply love, love in spite of myself. Now if you are my wife—and a tenderly loved wife you will be—you will in a measure be dependent upon your husband, and that is very sweet to a self-willed man like myself. Perhaps in time I can even make it sweet to you." (281)

They enter the château, and the caretaker, Benjamin Franklin, lights a fire and brings food. Ford then offers his own version of Percival's earlier toast: "Here's to you all, charming vanished ladies of the past . . . may you each have every honor in the picturesque, powdered, unorthographic age to which you belong, and never by any possibility step over into ours!" (282). Katharine protests that "that last touch has spoiled the whole." A conversation ensues concerning Ford's faults, which Katharine summarizes for him: "You are narrow, prejudiced; you do not believe in progress of any kind. You would keep women down with an iron hand" (284). She does not mention his own egotism, which she recognizes later, when Ford reveals that he knew Percival would never marry her. Katharine's courage fails, and she cries: "It is too much. . . . you wait until I am rejected, cast aside; and then you come and win from me an avowal of my love, telling me afterwards—*afterwards*—" (286–287). The last scene in the story takes place in the Fords' library, near New York, where a watercolor of the Château of

Coppet hangs above the works of Corinne, arranged perfectly on the shelf below.

On one level "At the Château of Corinne" dramatizes the falling off of women's culture following the Civil War due to the manifold changes in society. In times past Katharine would have been able to find a fertile, supportive environment within a circle of other women. This tradition has degenerated, however, as the roster of Katharine's companions suggests. First, gushing Cousin Sylvia, who admires Mme de Staël indiscriminately and finds pleasure in the regularity of her own wax flower creations and displeasure in her pedestrian last name, Pitcher (suggestive of traditional women's domestic duties), is continually ill, implying the fading strength of True Womanhood. Like other male-identified women in the world of women's culture, she reads not *Corinne,* the text of female genius, but *Childe Harold.* Only in the privacy of her boudoir does she read what male culture would insist is a more pedestrian woman's novel, a work by Charlotte Yonge.

Perhaps even sillier is Cousin H. Walpole, who tries to pass himself off as a more famous H. Walpole and who, by virtue of his advanced age, neither threatens nor contributes to the vitality of the feminine social structure. Lorimer Percival, whose name signals his romantic personality and suggests an inefficacy of action in the male world, is also an interloper on women's culture, further diluting its strength. As Ford says, he is effeminate: he is a woman who is not one, a subversive male in a women's culture setting.

Katharine's world, then, one in which women's culture is primary, lacks vitality, comprising as it does weaklings and old women. No wonder she looks to Coppet for solace, for it is only there that she can recover the lost companionship of others like her. She and Mme de Staël are sister exiles: Corinne a physical exile from France because of a political disagreement with Napoleon, and Katharine an emotional and intellectual exile from a disappearing world of women's culture and from a society where Benjamin Franklins and their bourgeois values rule rather than serve female genius.

Into this dying world rides John Ford, an all-business, no-nonsense man's man, as his two-syllable spondaic name suggests. He is the representative of the heterosocial world that will penetrate and extinguish women's culture. He disregards social grace and the feelings of others, exercises little imagination, believes that appearance and reality are synonymous. His drive is toward total control, and very like Henry James's American, Christopher Newman, he intends to buy it. After finding Katharine wet and bedraggled, he announces that although he finds her penchant for too-small shoes ridiculous, he will nonetheless grant her twelve pairs a year to make her happy. His competition for the young widow is not really Lorimer Percival: such a relationship would strike him as unnatural, as lesbian. His real competition, his only real threat, is Mme de Staël, whom he views as masculine, with her turban and big feet, conventional symbols of masculinity.

In winning Katharine, Ford takes her from her women's culture world of nature into his library, the male bastion, near the masculine commercial capital of New York. It is here that both Katharine, metaphorically, and Mme de Staël, literally, are brought into line. Both had at least been supported by women's culture, weak though it may have been. Here in a heterosocial world, they are alone. The works of "that eloquent authoress and noble woman" are "ranged by themselves," and Katharine languishes in an alien environment as Woolson signals at the conclusion when Ford, in conversation with an unnamed visitor, addresses Katharine only "by-the-way" (287). Both Katharine and her idol, Mme de Staël, now exist in an uncompromising, commercial, heterosocial world, and so are further exiled.

Both women had been born into generations of transition if not downright upheaval, Mme de Staël coming of age during the French Revolution, and Katharine Winthrop during the American Civil War. Madelyn Gutwirth suggests this accident of birth as a cause for the marginalization of Mme de Staël: "Born into the Enlightenment, temperamentally attuned to the modern rather than the ancient, Mme de Staël must have been at some loss as to where to find appropriate models. No modern heroine existed that even suggested what she had it in mind to portray: feminine genius."[9] This may also explain the lack of respect generally given the works of Mme de Staël. Only recently has her work been weighed, as Percival suggests, with new balances. But even Ellen Moers must assume a reputation tarnished by contemporary critical standards, and she begins her chapter in *Literary Women* on the myth of Corinne with "Let us try to take *Corinne* seriously."[10]

The same fate of being caught without an identity between strong generations befalls Corinne's admirer, Katharine Winthrop, a writer on the wrong side of both True and New Womanhood. Certainly more modern than her domestic, male-identified cousin Sylvia, who does little more than make her wax water lilies and read *Childe Harold*, Katharine is still no New Woman. She publishes anonymously, for example, like many domestic writers of an earlier generation. This fact, coupled with her desire for approval, suggests that she suffers from what Ellen Moers calls "the dilemma of Corinne as Mme de Staël": "the desire for fame stimulates her mind, but reason counsels obscurity."[11] Moreover, Katharine Winthrop's work seems to suffer from the same "defects" as Corinne's, especially in its coloring, which Ford deems exaggerated: "Reading it," he had remarked, "one was cloyed with color" (267). (So, too, runs one explanation of the weakness of the local colorists, with whom Woolson is nearly always grouped.) Like Mme de Staël, Katharine has no models but Corinne herself. When, at the end, she finds herself adrift in the world, having lost her fortune, she must turn to a traditional solution and marry Ford, for unlike Mme de Staël and Corinne, she is not independently wealthy. Her sacrifice is great: she must give up her art. Indeed, in the closing section of the story she is addressed, but having been silenced, she cannot respond. She becomes invisible, suffering the condition that had threatened madness in Corinne.

Although we neither see nor hear her, we can sense her anguish because of her identification with Mme de Staël. For example, both women are at early ages bonded to much older men in marriages of convenience; both, though still in their youths when their respective narratives begin (Corinne is twenty-six, Katharine twenty-seven), are fast approaching thirty, a traditional watershed year in a woman's life. Both receive company (Coppet was well known to host illustrious visitors); both are characterized by the term *enthusiasm*, the adjectival form being applied to both heroines; both are attended by older maiden aunts, who subscribe to the values of women's culture and act as foils to their ambitions (the same is true in *Aurora Leigh*); both are exiled to patriarchal spaces, Corinne to her father's estate at Coppet and Katharine to her husband's library near New York, punished like children in an effort to stop their subversive games.

More broadly, however, "At the Château of Corinne" is the story of Everywoman's struggle to attain independent identity by asserting her self. Artistic achievement becomes a metonymy of the woman's coming to identity; the artist, an example of a fully realized individual, the best womanhood can offer. Such achievement and personal integrity are denied Katharine Winthrop. Traditional women's writing images of entrapment, enclosure, and anger dominate her narrative in a way that they do not in *Corinne* because, in that myth, the truth of the heroine's wealth has made her free.

Katharine Winthrop's narrative revises yet again the dramatic narrative of enclosure and escape, which Susan Gubar and Sandra M. Gilbert see operating in nineteenth-century literature by women.[12] In these works, houses function as primary symbols of women's imprisonment. As an opening description reveals, Katharine's residence is as surely her jail as any house in women's literature:

> Mrs. Winthrop's villa was not one of the larger residences. It was an old-fashioned square mansion, half Swiss, half French, ending in a high-peaked roof, which came slanting sharply down over several narrowed half-stories, indicated by little windows like dove-perches—four in the broadest part, two above, then one winking all alone under the peak. On the left side a round tower, inappropriate but picturesque, joined itself to the square outline of the main building; the round tower had also a peaked roof, which was surmounted by a contorted ornament of iron somewhat resembling a letter S. Altogether the villa was the sort of a house which Americans are accustomed to call "quaint." (237)

This opening description will bear explication. First, the residence is small, physical diminutiveness being a quality peculiar to women's writing, particularly in the nineteenth century.[13] It is, however, a solid structure, square, yet apparently divided against itself in its undecided parentage, half-Swiss, half-French. It is half cool and calm (as the Swiss are stereotypically depicted)—in other words, masculine;

half romantic and emotional (following the traditional reading of the French character)—in other words, feminine. Similarly, Katharine Winthrop embodies both the extravagant French imagination and the practical Swiss mind that runs against freedom of creative expression.

Next, the narrow, high-peaked roof violently pierces the sky, in a phallic suggestion. This roof dominates "narrowed half-stories, indicated by little windows," images of diminution, attenuation, reduced vision, and access to light, suggesting knowledge or imagination. These little windows resembling dove perches remind the reader that the female bird-spirit of freedom and imagination is imprisoned there. And if, on the uppermost story, isolated from the rest, is one lonely window, it is nonetheless dominated by the masculine triumphal peak.

The structure also features a round tower, traditionally a symbol of the metaphysical, or the artistic consciousness, an emblem, in this story, of Katharine's talent. Here it is not only apparently an appendage to the main building (it "joined itself to the square outline of the main building" as the feminine must join itself to the masculine, and as Katharine must join herself to Ford), but it is also considered "inappropriate." Even the tower is dominated by a peaked roof, but a symbol of the entire ediface—which verily declares itself a symbol thereby—surmounts all, this "a contorted ornament of iron somewhat resembling a letter S." The S of selfhood, of de Staëlian ambition, is contorted, twisted; it suggests, as does the derivation of the word *contort,* torture and deformation. Katharine Winthrop's home, then, is just one of these houses that fill the landscape of women's writing where the entrapped artist is victimized by patriarchal domination.

Indeed, the heroine has access to water, that medium that offers others, like Edna Pontellier in *The Awakening* or Maggie Tulliver in *The Mill on the Floss,* escape, freedom, choice, or a return to the primal mother through death. For Katharine, however, instead of freedom, the lakeside represents a margin, a barrier that further limits her ambition. For even the lake has been appropriated by John Ford, who arrives at the villa by water, rowing to the water steps: the only time Katharine goes out on the lake is for a midnight row instigated by Ford. Even his name, Ford, signals his agenda, for, according to traditional myth, "Every animal that rises out of a ford is a representation of the forces of the unconscious, like some demonic being."[14] Ford is that Eternal Masculine force that invades women's culture, here represented by the lake, to take possession of the female artist.[15] In fact, all of the water, that age-old symbol of the Eternal Feminine, in "At the Château of Corinne," from that implied by Sylvia Pitcher's patronymic to the dampness and rain chased away by Benjamin Franklin's ministrations to the watercolor sketch of Coppet that hangs in the Fords' library, is appropriated by male power.

Mme de Staël did not fare much better in her father's house, also located on the banks of Lac Leman. The Château of Corinne, Coppet itself, also presents an image of confinement, suggesting a kinship between Katharine and Corinne. Like Katharine's home, the Necker château is plain, old-fashioned: "built round three sides of a square, a court-yard within. From the end of the south side a long, irregular wing of lower outbuildings stretches towards the road, ending in a thickened, huddled knot along its margin, as though the country highway had refused to allow aristocratic encroachments, and had pushed them all back with determined hands" (252). All of the shutters are "tightly closed" against the world. On the grounds is a garden that "stretched back behind the house for some distance, shut in by a high stone wall. A long, straight alley, shaded by even rows of trees, went down one side like a mathematical line; on the other there was some of the stiff landscape-gardening of the last century. In the open space in the centre was a moss-grown fish-pond, and near the house a dignified little company of clipped trees" (255).

In many ways, the extended description of Coppet reminds one of Katharine Winthrop's villa: it, too, is an enclosure, a prison, as implied by Mme de Staël's history of exile and Woolson's insistence on the knot image, a symbol of "binding and fettering."[16] Yet even while Coppet is walled and shuttered, it is not itself a square: rather, the possibility of issue (or escape) is assured since it is built on three instead of four sides of a square, with an inner courtyard, suggesting the female sphere of influence, in the middle. The garden, however, is completely walled, offering a pond, a round female image to counter the long, straight, mathematical line of phallic trees bordering the alley. Like Katharine's villa, Coppet is located at the edge of the lake, as suggested by Corinne's patronymic, *Edgermond*—"edge of the world."

Unlike Katharine, herself, however, Mme de Staël, who becomes Corinne, could transcend all boundaries, even the threshold of identity, unconstrained by a man. Her independent income allowed her some choice in her destiny, as suggested by the landscape and physical disposition of her residence in exile, as described by Constance Fenimore Woolson. Her wealth permitted this genuine woman of genius to costume herself in eccentric turbans and capes and to assert her individualism rather than to bow to patriarchally decreed custom. She could even choose the veil if she wished, as she does when she enters a convent for a period of retreat, for she was empowered with the right of purchase rather than being herself an economic commodity. Not a chattel to be bought and sold, Mme de Staël could become an exemplary woman of art and power through financial independence.

Katharine Winthrop cannot direct her own destiny and so cannot be the model woman of genius. Although, like her heroine Corinne, she is full of enthusiasm and quick with a witty remark, her financial status prevents her from attaining her ambition. When she loses her fortune, she also loses Percival. The veils and mirrors, paintings and statues, that Mme de Staël—and the fictional Corinne, the tour guide—can perform with because of her financial security, insist on Katharine's own entrapment in patriarchal culture. Her veils result not from self-assertion, but rather from anger. Recently Jean Baker Miller, in writing of women's fear of power, has commented that "anger is an especially important part of powerlessness. Remaining in a powerless position can be a refuge from one's fearsome anger."[17] Katharine Winthrop's real and metaphorical veiling on several occasions is attributable to anger, first when Ford reviles the idea of great poetry's coming from women—"She was so unlike herself, veiled in that deep, steady, painful blush" (269)—next after Ford begs her to marry him and the veiling blush reappears, and again when she asks Ford about his "principal faults" and shields "her face from the heat of the fire with her riding gauntlets" in a veiling motion (283). In one of the final scenes, after Katharine has accepted her marital fate, she rises and goes to the mirror to adjust her riding hat, an accessory almost sure to have been understood by Woolson's readers as having a veil.

At only one point in the story does an image from women's writing suggesting freedom and artistic inspiration appear: after Ford proposes, "one very wet and bedraggled little bird, who was in the tree above" chirrups "one note quite briskly" (279) and moves to arrange "his soaked feathers" (280). The bird obviously represents Katharine, the poet, yet it is important to note that the bird does not engage in a lengthy song: it has not been given the encouragement to create, inspired to produce poetry. Rather, the bird chirps once, briskly, to acknowledge the good fortune that his physical needs will be met, then returns to the business of caring for the needs of the flesh rather than the spirit.

Without money in a world that, bound by social convention, requires either money or a husband, Katharine is at risk. Her artistry, emblematic of women's creative capacity, does not endow her with the wherewithal to challenge the patriarchy. Rather, her creative capacity is a liability enabling others to perceive her as a weak, or "emotional," or "enthusiastic" woman. The two men who want to marry her are eager to appropriate her as a commodity. In this way, "At the Château of Corinne" further revises Mme de Staël's narrative. Madelyn Gutwirth has noticed that "the *Edinburgh Review* saw that the interest of Mme de Staël's fictions was 'founded on the inherent and almost inevitable heartlessness of polished men. The impression which they leave upon the mind is both painful and humiliating.' *Corinne* condemns the incapacity of men to integrate their emotional life and their moral imagination. It condemns the reserve that makes a gulf of a small breach between people and especially between couples."[18] Like Corinne's lovers, both of Katharine Winthrop's suitors are heartless and polished, but the heroine is unable to recognize her artistry as a valid element in her identity.

The names of Katharine's pursuers offer clues to her predicament. Lorimer Percival is a dangerous fop attracted to Katharine because of her fortune. Despite his apparent encouragement of her talents, his patriarchal nature offers her little genuine help. That they meet in the masculine environment of the library signals the fatherly role he has fashioned for himself. Like many fathers of the day, he would educate his "daughter" among his books, penned by the best male minds. Moreover, his first name, *Lorimer,* means "bit or bridle maker"; his last has even more explicit sexual implications, for *Perce-val* means "pierce the valley," a metaphor for violent sexual conquest. His family's emblem is fire, an agent whose power, appropriated by Ford, is destined to destroy the heroine. The medieval sound of the name *Lorimer Percival* further implies the patriarchal, bellicose nature of the man hidden behind the "effeminate" exterior.

The name and the man John Ford, though more modern sounding to our ears, do not hold any more freedom for Katharine Winthrop than does Lorimer Percival. Woolson's telling us that he is the son of a woman named Mary suggests that he is the very embodiment of a patriarchal order decreed by Christian myth. Or, to view it another way, Ford is the figure that appears in the woman's *Künstlerroman* as the "Eternal Masculine." As Linda Huf explains, he is "a would-be domestic dictator who through his strength or his weakness prevents the artist from working."[19]

For contemporary readers, no doubt, Ford's name suggests the commercial nature of Henry Ford, the great industrialist. And indeed, John Ford does have an exploitative material, commercial nature, though it is Percival's father who has been the railroad baron. Ford seems jealous of the fortune he thinks Percival enjoys as a result of his father's success: "There is nothing in the world so powerful as steam. If I only had more, I too might be a poet. Or if my father had had more, I too might have enjoyed a fortune" (261). He thinks everyone shares his values, and to convince Katharine to marry him, he appeals to a materialism he assumes she harbors by offering as a bribe twelve new pairs of shoes. The closing scene in his library reaffirms for the reader Ford's bourgeois orientation.

Yet another way to explain John Ford and to suggest the danger he poses for Katharine Winthrop is through feminist psychoanalytic theory. It appears that John Ford exemplifies the narcissistic impulse, which Luce Irigaray describes as "aggressive toward the 'object' that it tortures systematically whenever possible, that it would like to eliminate when its needs have been served or when its strength no longer relies on dominating and possessing the object."[20] Furthermore, this impulse "is always at war in order to have things, and have more things, and take things from others; in order to accumulate and build up capital, losing nothing."[21] Women are the commodity, femininity "*the image, the specular production-reproduction. Which is also speculative. The eye will ensure the recovery. . . . The mirror will idealize the product* that it will have introduced both into the field of optics and into an economy of reproduction. . . . Possession is ensured, mastered, eternalized just as it is always already re-produced and therefore reproducible."[22] Katharine becomes for Ford a mere reflection of his own desire, an ambition he sees as nothing if not attainable. As he comments, "When one is grown . . . there is very little that is absolutely out of reach" (257).

Perhaps more than any evidence, Woolson's own rhetoric of the mirror confirms Ford's threatening, narcissistic personality. In "At the Château of Corinne" a mirror scene occurs at two points, the second recalling the first. The first occasion takes place after Katharine has admitted to being a writer, after Ford's statement that he pities literary women. On asking whether he knows that she writes, she looks at "*his image* in the glass" (264, my emphasis). In the paragraph immediately preceding, "She had crossed the room to examine an old mirror made of squares of glass, welded together by little leaden frames, which had once been gilded" (264). In other words, although she is examining the mirror and logically, her own image would appear therein, Katharine can see nothing but Ford since she exists only as a reflection of him. Moreover, the mirror into which she has been fixed as his reproduced image is, in fact, a small prison, made as it is of squares of glass joined by "little leaden frames." The image of the mirror foreshadows the confinement of the marital state for Katharine and women like her: although the leaden frames are now visible, they "had once been gilded." Appropriately, the only passage of Katharine's writing of which Ford approves is "a charming little description somewhere—about going out on the Campagna to gather the wild narcissus" (265). The mythic Narcissus, we remember, had been turned into a flower after falling in love, as Ford does here, with his own reflection.

In the echoing mirror scene, "He watched her in the glass a moment, then drew her away" (285). If one pursues the same line of reasoning, it might appear that Ford is here imprisoned in Katharine's image; however, the point seems to be that the woman can never see herself in the mirror. Whereas she looks at him in the first scene, prior to the loss of her fortune and thus her power, by the end she is located and bound by his mirror, Ford's own speculative economy. In this last mirror scene, Ford has consolidated his control: "His, surely, is the voice of the looking glass, the patriarchal voice of judgment that rules . . . every woman's . . . self-evaluation. He it is who decides, first, that his consort is 'the fairest of all,' and then, as she becomes maddened, rebellious, witchlike, that she must be replaced by his angelically innocent and dutiful daughter, a girl who is therefore defined as 'more beautiful still.'"[23]

Indeed, it is Ford's voice that we hear. Kinglike, he decrees: "You will write no more" (285). He proceeds to tell her that he had known about the broken engagement but that he had never really understood her attraction to the effeminate Percival in the first place: "I suspect it was because he flattered what you thought your literary talent" (286). The rhetoric of the mirror serves to reinforce Ford's narcissism, to elucidate his character flaws and thus the hopeless situation in which Katharine Winthrop finds herself, that of a penniless widow. Henry James recognized the sad situation of women like her: "It is a very dismal truth," he wrote in "Modern Women," "that the only hope of most women, at the present moment, for a life worth the living, lies in marriage. . . . But to our minds there is nothing comical in the situation."[24] Katharine Winthrop is well aware of her position in life: she must capitulate to Ford for reasons of physical security.

Ranging over cultures and centuries in its intertextuality, "At the Château of Corinne" implicates not only Mme de Staël and her creation Corinne, Constance Woolson and her creation Katharine Winthrop, Elizabeth Barrett Browning and Aurora Leigh, and the myth of Snow White—sisters in their repression by the patriarchal societies which they inhabit—but also the mythic Cinderella. Although Charles Perrault finally wrote down the tale in 1647, doubtless the structure had been subconsciously institutionalized in Western thought long before. Just as that narrative turns on the point (size) of a shoe, so does "At the Château of Corinne."

In Perrault's story as it has come down to us, the poor stepdaughter of a social-climbing matron with daughters of her own is visited by an apparition, born of imagination—a fairy godmother, who clothes the girl in splendid garments, complete with glass footwear suitable for attending the prince's ball. At midnight, however, the spell is broken, and Cinderella flees the ball, losing one of her slippers in the process. The prince vows to wed the woman whose foot fits into the slipper. Try as the wicked stepsisters will, they cannot force their big feet into the diminutive slipper. For Cinderella, of course, the fit is perfect, and once she has been found, she and the prince live happily ever after.

It makes sense that the Freudians like this story, for they read the foot as a phallic symbol. Cinderella, however, is a True Woman, and her phallic feature is much diminished. To be made complete, she need only wait for the prince to produce his/her glass slipper, a symbol of the female sex organ. In this way, he entraps and appropriates her. The Eternal Masculine, the prince, the son of the king, wants none of Cinderella's more masculine sisters of the big feet, who threaten by their assertiveness.

Katharine Winthrop is another Cinderella. Her shoes are "little boots of dark cloth like the [riding] habit, slender, dainty, and made with thin soles" (283). Her feet are tiny, as we know when Ford suggests that they stop to buy her a new pair in a "children's size" (280). Corinne, he has noted, must have worn "a much larger pair" (282). The fact is that Katharine cannot fill Corinne's shoes, that she is forced to depend on the prince to provide shoes (twelve pairs) for her. Like Cinderella, and unlike Mme de Staël, she lacks financial means: her feet are in reduced circumstances. At the end of "At the Château of Corinne" Katharine Winthrop is even more a *cendrillon:* she is fixed in the mirror, a piece of glass silvered on the back to reflect the sun (son), a piece of glass with the capacity to burn. Indeed, this mirror, the symbol of the imagination, is appropriated by the materialistic Ford, who burns the creative capacity out of his wife. She begins to burn in the last scenes, when, as a result of her reduced circumstances, she is forced to accept Ford's suit, as the several references to her flushed complexion and her red cheeks suggest. Finally, her creative ability to use language is voided after her expression of anguish. "You wait until I have lost my fortune and am overwhelmed; you wait until I am rejected, cast aside; and then you come and win from me an avowal of my love, telling me afterwards—*afterwards*—" (286–287) are the last words the reader hears from Katharine though the narrative continues for five paragraphs more, including a scene in which she not only is present but also is addressed.

But "At the Château of Corinne" was not published until seven years after it was written. Perhaps its implications and its position in Woolson's oeuvre, following as it does close on the heels of "'Miss Grief,'" left Woolson depressed. For the marriage that concludes the story is unlike Mme de Staël's marriage of convenience, which gave her the freedom that the marital state granted a woman of her degree. Rather, Katharine Winthrop's marriage is one of financial necessity. Whereas Mme de Staël, even in exile, received company and maintained an active social life, writing, dancing, and entertaining, Katharine Winthrop is truly isolated. Taken under her husband's control, put into his library, she, like the works of her heroine, is ranged separately on a shelf, a collectible, a conversation piece, an objet d'art displayed for the purpose of eliciting from her husband the clever sort of commentary that concludes the narrative. This paradigmatic story of female literary artistry in the last decades of the nineteenth century, originally written in 1880, did not appear until October 1887. We may wonder what led Constance Fenimore Woolson to unearth in 1887 a manuscript she had written seven years earlier.

Her reading of *Aurora Leigh,* another text of female artistry, this from the mid-nineteenth century, along with her own residence in Italy, the setting for *Corinne,* probably led Woolson to resurrect "At the Château of Corinne." From 1 January of that year until the fall of 1889 she leased Villa Brichieri at Bellosguardo in Florence, the same villa the Brownings had visited many years earlier. Woolson writes of her happiness in inhabiting the historic establishment in a letter to her former teacher Miss Linda Guilford dated 1 March 1887:

> I wish I could show you my view here. Take down "Aurora Leigh," turn to the seventh Book, and find the passage beginning "I found a house at Florence on the hill of Bellosguardo," etc., and you have a good description, save that poor Mrs. Browning—who almost never left her house down in the

crowded town (Casa Guidi)—seems not to have been familiar with our second view here, namely the view down "the sweet Val d'Arno" toward the west. From the north and east sides of my villa I have the view described in "Aurora Leigh."[25]

Woolson's sister Clara Benedict explained the villa's historic distinction in a letter to their niece, Kate Mather: "It is the only one [villa] that Mrs. Browning entered, and in my parlour is a sofa upon which she sat once for three hours, as she looked off upon the same view that we exclaim over every day, and where she thought of that lovely description of it in 'Aurora Leigh.' "[26] Mrs. Benedict then notes that she has christened this sofa the "Browning shrine."[27] For Browning, through the influence of Mme de Staël and Corinne, and, it is clear, for Woolson herself, Italy came to be "the nurturing *matria* of a 'woman of genius,' " and Aurora Leigh became another Corinne.[28] For Woolson, thinking of "Aurora Leigh" in 1887 would have directly implicated Mme de Staël and *Corinne, or Italy.*

In the nineteenth century the patriarchal establishment was ready for neither Barrett Browning nor de Staël. It was likewise unprepared to grant credence to either Aaronna Moncrief or Katharine Winthrop. In the works of the first two, the artist cannot pursue both love and art: Aurora Leigh chooses love, figuring this greater than art; Corinne dies. Of Woolson's creations, Miss Grief, too, dies; Katharine Winthrop, an intertextual embodiment of them all, is effectively silenced by a marriage to which she sacrifices both love and art. Woolson had written that hearing a snatch of the Ronsard lyrics "*le temps s'en va, le temps s'en va, ma belle*" had recalled the story to her seven years after she had written it.[29] These nostalgic phrases had perhaps reminded her that she, like Katharine Winthrop, was a woman writer who had been destined by accident of time and birth to give up if not art, then the possibility of love.

SEVEN • "THE STREET OF THE HYACINTH": THE CONVENTIONS OF FAITH

Woolson's letter of 4 August 1882 from Baden-Baden to E. C. Stedman approves of his criticism of her story "The Street of the Hyacinth," but she protests, "Why do you accuse me of putting real persons into my pages? Real persons are seldom usable in a novel" (Stedman Papers); or, she might have added, in any piece of fiction. One could argue that the lady doth protest too much. After all, Woolson, like Ethelinda Faith Macks, the protagonist of "The Street of the Hyacinth," had arrived in Rome with a letter of introduction to the literary man of the hour; he—Raymond Noel in the story and Henry James in reality—squired the heroine around the galleries; both male writers prefer to call the protagonists by their middle names; both women have brothers who attempt to make their fortunes in California but die trying. Or, if one is uncomfortable with autobiographical argument, one may argue the anxiety of influence, for elements of "The Street of the Hyacinth" do resemble strategies from *Daisy Miller:* both narratives are presented for the most part from the limited perspective of an unreliable third-person narrator; both feature naive American girls with inappropriate mothers; both narrators are involved with foreign ladies. In either reading, James and his relationship with Woolson take top billing.

A more illuminating approach to the story is to regard it in the context of Woolson's earlier efforts at artist-heroine fiction, particularly the earlier "'Miss Grief'" and the earlier-written though later published "At the Château of Corinne." First published in the *Century Magazine* (May–June 1882) and reprinted in the posthumous collection *The Front Yard and Other Italian Stories,* "The Street of the Hyacinth" is more than just "a good piece of work" though "not entirely successful because of the shift in Faith's attitude."[1] Indeed, Rayburn S. Moore's evaluation of merit cannot begin to account for the attraction of the story to a feminist critic. He writes:

> Since it has little plot and therefore small need for such devices as tension, suspense, and denouement, it has the quality of a leisurely sketch that introduces its characters in an appropriate Old World setting and allows them to grow within the context of a dramatic contrast between the new and the old, between innocence and experience.[2]

Rather, the story is part of the triad of Woolson's fiction that works through the artist-heroine's plight in a changing world. Its very title evokes a myth that recalls both the title and the plot of "'Miss Grief.'" In the story of Apollo and Hyacinthus, the flower that springs from the youth's blood has six bell-shaped petals on which can be deciphered the letters *AI,* Greek for "grief." More important, however, in Greek myth, Hyacinthus was slain by Apollo, his teacher, in the same way that Miss Grief and Ettie Macks are in effect silenced by their mentors. Further, as in "At the Château of Corinne," at the tragic conclusion of "The Street of the Hyacinth" the artist-heroine capitulates to a less bright, less energetic man. Her downfall means marriage, and for her, marriage means silence rather than celebration. Like Aaronna Moncrief and Katharine Winthrop, the two heroines who precede her, Ethelinda Faith Macks is an artist, specifically a visual artist whose production is appropriated by a conservative male establishment dedicated to maintaining the status quo. Ettie, like Aaronna and Katharine (and Mme de Staël), represents a liberal, liberating power—politically, socially, artistically—and, as such, is a threat to men like Raymond Noel here, the Balzacian narrator of "'Miss Grief,'" and John Ford, who plays Napoleon to Katharine's Corinne. The power of the patriarchy, however, invalidates her attempt to reverse the conservative paradigm.

As Sharon Dean notes, "Woolson's story seems straightforward enough."[3] Faith begins as a naive American girl, newly arrived in Europe to pursue what we learn is her "small talent" for drawing and her big crush on one of the most popular writers on artistic topics. The writer flirts with her a little, accompanying her on several gallery tours, pushes her off on a colleague, and leaves town to pursue a cultured continental woman. When he returns, he finds that the young woman has not only made a name for herself as a schoolteacher, but also earned the love of two men: a titled gentleman and her respected drawing teacher. Having grown in social grace, she is now attractive to him, and Noel pursues her until, faced with the prospect of being left homeless, she is no longer able to resist his advances. Dean reads the story as a romance in which Faith, though apparently naive, is actually pursuing Noel: that she calculatedly refuses both the count and the art teacher because neither possesses the combination of money and culture she finds in the writer. The story, Dean explains, may be understood "in terms of betrayal and entrapment."[4] It seems to me, however, that Ettie—or Faith—presents a revolutionary option, a feminist mode of existence that runs counter to the patriarchal world in which her antagonist operates. For the story of "The Street of the Hyacinth" to be told, she must be brought to her knees. Artifice must subsume nature.

Ettie does meet her "downfall" as Noel puts it: thus, he must present the narrative. Indeed, the story belongs to Raymond Noel rather than to Ettie, as is made readily apparent by the rhetoric of the opening passages, which creates what turn out to be artificial images only to have them yanked from the reader's gaze with a disclaimer, as if to say "I'm the one with the power of the narrative, and I can do what I will." The first paragraph, for example, presents the Street of the Hyacinth in its narrow, winding, untidy condition: "Two vehicles meeting there could pass only by grazing the doors and windows on either side, after the usual excited whipcracking and shouts which make the newcomer imagine, for his first day or two, that he is proceeding at a perilous speed through the sacred city of the soul" (144). The succeeding sentence, however, destroys the image: "But two vehicles did not often meet in the street of the Hyacinth. It was not a thoroughfare, not even a convenient connecting link" (144). One of the next images presents the street's inhabitants tossing refuse from the windows into city refuse carts: "No one but an unreasonable foreigner would dream of objecting" (144). The following sentence once again disqualifies the image: "But unreasonable foreigners seldom entered the street of the Hyacinth" (144). It is in this way that Noel's later admitted hypocrisy is revealed and he joins the literary fraternity whose members number people like the narrator of " 'Miss Grief.' " Even the last sentence of the narrative reinforces this pattern of assertion and denial that characterizes Noel and points up his unreliability. Through his consciousness we hear his friend Mrs. Lawrence sigh: "It is the most fortunate thing in the world . . . that Mrs. Spurr is now confined to her bed for life, and is obliged to wear mourning" (183). Then, in characteristic manner, the text recants: "But Mrs. Spurr is not confined to her bed; she drives out with her daughter whenever the weather is favorable. She wears black, but is now beginning to vary it with purple and lavender" (183).

Noel is full of "just mere talk," as Ettie puts it more than once; he is a social being who uses "conventional remarks as filling-up" (153). A casual comment made as a "filling up" reveals more about Noel than he suspects: "I fear, Miss Macks, that writers are seldom good illustrations of their own doctrines" (153). As a writer, he is indeed fearful of the silence his words supplement: that silence is the space women inhabit that only *l'écriture féminine* is appropriate to describe.[5]

As his language reveals, Noel fears the dark, primitive side of women, the silent and unnamed that underlies the conventions he must naturalize in order to maintain control. Therefore, he must seize power and reshape situations so as to defuse the threats they pose. Ettie Macks is so utterly frank that on meeting Noel for the first time, she reprimands him for his tardiness in paying the call. He is "thus put at once upon the defensive" (145). To counter Ettie's remark Noel offers his own thrust in return to her supposition that "society here is all finished off—there are no rough ends" (145). Noel's reply reads like a sexual threat: "There are ends. If not rough, they are often sharp" (145). Somewhat later, he is able to score points and seize control by renaming her to suit his desire. Her name is actually *Ethelinda,* an old Germanic compound meaning "noble serpent"; we can easily understand why Noel prefers the name *Faith,* which is, Ettie says, "so old fashioned" (159). First, her given name suggests a usurpation of male power in its mythic reference to the serpent; second, the name *Faith* complements his own *Noel* and so confirms his identity; and third, as an old-fashioned name, *Faith* harkens back to a time when women observed more rigorously the social codes set up for them by men.[6]

Raymond Noel is comfortable with and can condone only what convention dictates. His speech must be filled with courtesies, his women with a certain falsity he considers indispensible, for in his life custom rules. Convention, however, is flexible from his perspective, for it even allows for its own breakdown under specified conditions. For example, Ettie may meet Noel at various galleries because she is a student and "art students had, or took, privileges of their own in Rome" (161). He honors any convention either of social nicety or of artistic merit, such as the Pantheon, uncritically. Indeed he need not submit any social convention to a rigorous analysis to sense that it, as a time-honored habit, certifies his own power.

In his absolute reliance on what has preceded him—artistically, socially, politically, qualified by the fact that he must see it or feel it reinforced around him—Noel strikes us as a person without faith, as a faithless man: that is, he cannot submit himself to mysteries, cannot trust in something for which there is no proof or immediate validation. In this sense his name can be understood as nothing if not ironic: for he is not the light of the world (*Ray-mond*), not the proclamation of the promise of the salvation of mankind (*Noel,* a Christmas carol); he is rather the death knell of Ettie's artistic efforts. Darker mysteries of faith elude him. Although he is a popular writer, our impression is that textual moments, scenes of narrative *aporia* where the joy of textuality takes place, never appear in his art. As an artist, Noel is devoted to surface, refusing to recognize how it deconstructs itself even though he admits to being a hypocrite. He swears that art *is* real. His real love interest is described as "a charming product of the effects of finished cultivation and fashionable life upon a natural foundation of grace, wit, and beauty of the French kind. She was not artificial, because she was art itself. Real art is as real as real nature is natural" (162). Just whom is Noel trying to fool here?

Ettie Macks, however, is another story entirely. A country girl from the fictional town of Tuscolee Falls in the American "West," she does not conform to the conventions of femininity that Noel can understand and manipulate. Ettie is very much a New Woman, describing herself as enjoying "abruptness," "perfectly frank," apparently "conceited," with "a great deal of ambition" as well as determination. Unlike Noel, she is direct, reminding him that her narrative is drawn out only because he ought to "know absolutely the whole" (147). Moreover, she is intelligent, an assessment that calls into question the reliability of Noel's claim that Ettie was "unaware of any intrusion, or any exhorbitance in her demands" on his time (151).

Because she conforms so little to his internalized conventions of womanhood—embodying grace, a certain degree of falsity, passivity, and so on—Noel describes Ettie in conventionally male-gendered descriptions such as "sober" and "earnest." No wonder he balks at considering the possibility of her feeling desire for a man, which from his perspective would verge on the homosexual. Her declaration that she is at Noel's feet is "as impersonal as those which had preceded it" (153). Ettie tells Noel in no uncertain terms what she wants from him, as if to present herself as a counterexample to those male-identified women of the type Noel understands, who can be "so diffuse":

> "And so, then, first: I would like your opinion of all that I have done so far. I have brought everything with me to show you. Second: I want your advice as to the best teacher; I suppose there is a great choice in Rome. Third: I should be glad if you would give a general oversight to all I do for the next year. And last, if you would be so kind, I should much enjoy making visits with you to all the galleries and hearing your opinions again by word of mouth, because that is always so much more vivid, you know, than the printed page." (148)

Like Aaronna Moncrief, Ettie prefers oral presentation—a more connected, contextual form of communication; an unrecorded, nonhierarchical, and thus feminine language—to the written text of the artifact, which enters patriarchal culture. Like speech rather than text, Ettie insists on being the primary name giver, refusing "to *reflect any* one" (148). Her identity is that of an artist, as she explains to Noel: "In the lives of all—almost all—artists, I have noticed—haven't you?—that there comes a time when they have to live on hope and their own pluck more than upon anything tangible that the present has to offer. They have to take that risk. Well, I have taken it; I took it when we left America" (148).

Because of her devotion to her artistry, her focus on and approach to its development, Noel perceives Ettie as masculine. It is apparently her art that gives her the "slightly brown" complexion, appropriate only to a man; it is her art that fills her mind with so many "other things" that she does not consider how odd she looks. For Ettie pays no attention to fashion either in clothes or in hairstyles: her "compact coiffure, at a time when most feminine foreheads in Rome and elsewhere were shaded almost to the eyebrows by curling locks, and when the arched outline of the head was left unbroken, the hair being coiled in a low knot behind made Miss Macks look somewhat peculiar" (149) (not to mention threatening, given the snakelike coil of hair). The comment, made by some women passengers on the voyage over regarding Ettie's physical appearance, reflects Noel's own: " 'If that girl had more color, and if she was graceful, and if she was a little more womanly—that is, if she would not look at everything in such a direct, calm, impartial, impersonal sort of way"—in other words, if she would not respond like a man—"—she would be almost pretty' " (149). Even her name, pronounced in the Midwest fashion with its palatized *ts*, thus giving her the name *Eddie,* is perhaps another reason Noel objects to it, preferring instead the name *Faith.*

Hence the conflict between woman and artist. To be an artist, Ettie sacrifices her "femininity." But to survive in the world as a woman, she must deny her art. This archetypal conflict in the *Bildungsroman* and its subgenre the *Künstlerroman* is discussed by several critics, all of whom conclude that art and female gender norms are incompatible. Annis Pratt, for example, states that in the archetypal novel of female development, the young woman's dynamism and optimism oppose patriarchal limits, making the heroine's happiness an impossibility.[7] Art and woman's existence are mutually exclusive. As Linda Huf writes, the woman artist "must choose between her sexuality and her profession, between her womanhood and her work."[8] All of these critics decide that the female protagonist, particularly in the nineteenth century, is not able to become both artist and woman: the patriarchy won't let her.

Ettie tries to integrate her womanhood and her art during her walk with Noel following her marketing trip: "He was very fond of the old streets, and was curious to see whether she would notice the colors and outlines that made their picturesqueness. She noticed nothing but the vegetable stalls, and talked of nothing but her pictures" (154). Noel offers this detail to highlight Ettie's silliness; however, it throws into relief the difficulty the woman artist has reconciling her desire to care for loved ones and to create out of the self: to mother and at the same time to father. In fact, one of the aspects of Ettie that makes Noel most nervous is her art, particularly its "originality." Like Aaronna Moncrief, she has usurped the father's power to create, thus unsexing herself and casting herself as a threatening androgyne. As he admits, he ceases any pretense to gallantry with Ettie: "He talked to her not as though she was a boy exactly, or an old woman, but as though he himself was a relative of mature age—say an uncle of benevolent disposition and a taste for art" (162).

Ettie only becomes acceptable to Noel when her "lower emotions," those more appropriate to a woman than ambition and drive, overcome her. When she allows Noel to see two tears resulting from the frustration of caring for her ill mother in the absence of a servant, he finds them utterly charming, and before he leaves the city to follow his French paramour, he promises to send Ettie books. Only when he returns to find that Ettie has deserted her art and taken up schoolteaching, a profession appropriate for a young woman, is he completely taken with her. She is indeed greatly changed: "The old direct, wide glance was gone; gone also what he had called her overconfidence; she looked much older. On the other hand, there was more grace in her bearing, more comprehension of life in her voice and eyes. She was dressed as plainly as before; but everything, including the arrangement of her hair, was in the prevalent style" (167). Ethelinda Faith Macks has found that in order to live, she must earn a living: that is easier to do if one doesn't buck convention. Her transformation from artist to woman has brought monetary rewards in terms of her success as an English-speaking day governess and proposals from wealthy men: tangible rewards one need not accept on mere faith, rewards appropriate to a woman. Her faith has been replaced with "more grace in her bearing," that is, with artifice that assumes conventional approval.

Ettie repeats the fate scripted for Anne Brontë's paradigmatic heroine Helen Graham in *The Tenant of Wildfell Hall.* Both characters experience a downfall, suggested by the very title of Brontë's work and baldly stated at the end of Woolson's: "It [Ettie's marriage] was a great downfall of course; Noel always maintained that it was" (182). Like Helen, Ettie "must in some sense deny or conceal her own art, or at least deny the self-assertion implicit in her art."[9] For when she tells Noel on his return that she is no longer painting and he replies, quite qualifiedly, "Ah—isn't that rather a pity?" (167), she responds in a self-renunciatory, self-deprecatory manner: "A gleam of scorn filtered into the glance. 'You know it is not a pity,' she said" (168). Later, she further decries her earlier efforts: "The Western girl, the girl from Tuscolee! The girl who thought she could paint, and could not! The girl who knew so little of social rules that she made a fool of herself every time she saw you!" (176). Ettie recognizes, most painfully in the culmination of her self-scorn, that her happiness must be yoked to close study, not of art, but of social convention, partiarchally sanctioned social artifice. Ettie is forced to reject her frank, sober, straightforward approach to life—her life as a father-artist—and devote herself instead to life as a mother-nurturer, caring for her own mother in her illness, her brother in his final days, and Noel after he is injured by a fall from his horse.

Like Aaronna Moncrief and Katharine Winthrop, Ettie Macks, once she capitulates to a man, is silenced entirely, losing the power of self-assertion endowed her by her art and fading into the background. As in "At the Château of Corinne," the last words of the heroine here are a declaration of pure pain: "But, unless you will leave Rome, and—me, I cannot bear it longer" (182). And, like Katharine Winthrop, Ettie Macks is silenced: although the story continues for several more paragraphs following her capitulatory outburst, and although she is not only present but also addressed, she has forfeited the power of response. In this way, she is managed into obscurity, her art forever lost. She repeats the script her mother has taught her.

As in other artist-heroine fiction, the mother-daughter relationship in "The Street of the Hyacinth" is central. This strong bond between mothers and daughters is, as Grace Stewart notes, the "one common experience" informing all women's *Künstlerromanen:* "All women are daughters. Some are mothers. The mother/daughter relationship is often central to the novel of the artist as heroine."[10] We see the drive toward artistic expression passed on from mother to daughter throughout the nineteenth century, along with its by-product, alienation from woman's sphere. Finally, both mother and daughter are forced to choose between womanhood and art, between domestic security and creative fulfillment. Ready examples present themselves in the persons of Elizabeth Stuart Phelps, both mother and daughter, and in the daughter's creations: Avis Dobell, the painter; and her mother, the actress. Woolson's own mother, Hannah Cooper Pomeroy Woolson, was a gifted writer, as her letters and journals reveal. In fact, Woolson once asked her niece Katherine Livingston Mather for access to the manuscript volume of the recollections Mrs. Woolson had bequeathed her. "I have always thought that those of them that are not of a private nature, ought to be published; they are so very charming; they have a simplicity and reality of style that is very remarkable, and that my best efforts can never approach. . . . Of all the numerous 'Recollections' and 'Letters' I have read in the past ten years, I have found none more charmingly written than Mother's."[11] Although she wrote letters, diaries, and stories throughout her life, Hannah Cooper Pomeroy Woolson was devoted to her family, suffering greatly in her maternal role, losing five children before she herself died.

In all of these narratives, the daughter, gender-identified with her mother, attempts to fulfill both her and her mother's artistic ambitions and desires for self-expression; yet, she, too, is caught because she has internalized her own sex role. Such is the case with Ettie Macks, who has inherited her ability from her mother, Mrs. Spurr. Even before we see Mrs. Spurr and our suspicions are confirmed, we learn of her artistic pretensions. She has named her daughter Ethelinda Faith, "having thus combined euphony and filial respect—the first title being her tribute to aesthetics, the second her tribute to the memory of her mother" (145). In her daughter's name is represented the conflict of her—and other women artists'—life: art or womanhood. That the name *Ethelinda* represents her devotion to art further suggests why Noel dislikes the name. *Faith*, however, is appropriate since women are expected to exhibit filial respect without regard to tangible evidence that respect is deserved. Like other women artists, Mrs. Spurr by definition does not respect convention. She has never, for example, "possessed a visiting card in her life" (145). Neither does she use artifice to mask her linguistic origins: " 'It's this queer Eye-talian air,' " Mrs. Spurr complains. " 'You see I ain't used to it. Not but what I ain't glad to be here on Ettie's account—real glad. It's just what she needs and oughter have' "(165).

Mrs. Spurr's very physical presence, however, presents her at her most artistic and most powerful—and thus most threatening to the partiarchy. She commands space and presumes an unconventional freedom, which assaults societal expectation. Mrs. Spurr is the very incarnation of a wild zone woman's art—full of primitive primary color—that refuses to play by the rules:[12]

> Ettie's mother was a very portly matron of fifty-five, with a broad face, indistinct features, very high color, and a breathless, panting voice. Her high color—it really was her most noticeable feature—was surmounted by an imposing cap, adorned with large bows of scarlet ribbon; a worsted shawl, of the hue known as "solferino," decked her shoulders; under her low-necked collar reposed a bright blue necktie, its ends embroidered in red and yellow; and her gown was of a vivid dark green. But although her colors swore at each other, she seemed amiable. She was also voluble. (165)

At another point, Mrs. Spurr is dressed in five shades of red. Bright, sexual, threatening, she is the prototypical pro-creative principle—and her daughter's loudest cheerleader. Because her name, *Spurr*, implies strength and sexuality (and a masculine will to power) we understand why Noel cannot remember her name. He remembers, instead, *Stirrup,* a term that connotes subservience, as in the expression "to hold the stirrup" (OED). Mrs. Spurr is also a kind of madwoman in the attic, albeit a benign one. Or she is, at least, the author's or Ettie's double. As Gilbert and Gubar explain:

> Even the most apparently conservative and decorous women writers obsessively create fiercely independent characters who seek to destroy all the patriarchal structures which both their authors and their authors' submissive heroines seem to accept as inevitable. Of course, by projecting their rebellious impulses not into their heroines but into mad or monstrous women (who are suitably punished in the course of the novel or poem), female authors dramatize their own self-division, their desire both to accept the structures of patriarchal society and to reject them. What this means, however, is that the madwoman in literature by women is not merely, as she might be in male literature, an antagonist or foil to the heroine. Rather, she is usually in some sense the *author's* double, an image of her own anxiety and rage.[13]

Because neither Ettie nor Woolson is completely able to accept all that Mrs. Spurr represents and still survive in conventional late nineteenth-century culture, Mrs. Spurr is, on the evening of her seizing control from her daughter and traveling to America, made to fall ill, presumably losing her power of girth, and to become a mourning mother, thus forfeiting the power suggested by her idiosyncratic style of dress. She is the essential artist of the story, grieving wildly when her favored creation—the prodigal, ne'er-do-well son, John—dies. Unable to express herself in conventional artistic terms, she focuses her genius on filial artistry, as does her daughter, who remains, to use her own term, "faithful" to her mother.

The mother-daughter relationship that permeates not only this narrative, but most other stories of artist-heroines, takes on a mythic dimension as well. As many critics have noted, the Demeter-Persephone myth can offer an analogue to feminine artistic experience. In this myth Demeter, the goddess of agriculture and of the reproductive faculty, whose purpose is to feed and nurture, withholds her bounty from the earth while she mourns for her daughter, Persephone, who has been ravished by Pluto, ruler of the underworld. Finally, Zeus forces Pluto to release the maiden, but because Persephone has eaten a few pomegranate seeds, she must return to her husband for several months each year. In some versions of this myth Persephone is chosen to become Pluto's bride because she has threatened the authority of the gods, in the way Ettie threatens male authority early in the story. Demeter, the mourning mother, appears here as Mrs. Spurr, who mourns for a son rather than for a daughter.

Yet "The Street of the Hyacinth" is hardly an allegory: pieces and details do not match those of the Demeter-Persephone myth, though the mere setting of the story, in proximity to the Pantheon, suggests the bearing of myth on Woolson's narrative. Nonetheless, the plot of Woolson's story offers mythic resonances, for in the story as well as in the myth the Persephone figure becomes aware of male power and, separated from her mother and the power she represents, loses her own energy and spirit.[14] As Grace Stewart explains: "The woman artist born of a mother with suppressed or frustrated creative urges also struggles in the mother-daughter mold. Good or bad, the relationship energizes many women's novels and forms the core of most of their *Künstlerromanen.* In these autobiographical novels focusing on the difficulties or growth of the artist, the heroines must always wrestle with mothers, with daughters, or with their own identity in either role. The myth provides a clear view of the nature of those roles."[15]

Both the Demeter-Persephone myth and the hyacinth myth, the other narrative implied by the title of the story, suggest the fundamental conflict between nature and art, a conflict we have already seen at work and, in fact, a focal theme. Nature is stereotypically intuitive, instinctual, female, primeval, dangerous. Women control the natural world; men rule the world of manners, convention, artifice. The myth of Demeter and Persephone is primarily a story of grief and filial devotion, and the story of Apollo and Hyacinthus similarly focuses on sorrow and nurturance. The myths hold meaning for the natural world, explaining the cycle of growth and harvest, and the appearance and meaning of the hyacinth flower, respectively. These myths and their power will not be conventionalized; neither will they lie or dissemble.

Thus, the myths threaten the male-dominated civilization and must be brought under control. Part of the natural world, women are inappropriate artists. They should leave art to those who comprehend its conventions: those endowed with patriarchal power. At the beginning, Ettie is natural, frank, without falsity: this basic, powerful femininity Noel reads as an attempt to appropriate patriarchal options. She should be, as Ettie sarcastically recognizes, "very charming and obedient and sweet"—in other words, a conventional representative of man's idea of womankind (177).

Both mother and daughter, Demeter and Persephone—particularly Persephone—live in the wild zone, that figurative territory sacred to women and feared by men. As Edwin Ardener has argued, "Where society is defined by men, some features of women do not fit that definition. In rural societies the anomaly is experienced as a feature of the 'wild,' for the 'wild' is a metaphor of the non-social which in confusing ways is vouched for by the senses."[16] "The Street of the Hyacinth" is obviously that wild zone for Raymond Noel. We are told at the very beginning of the tale that the narrator is anxious about the territory. The street, after all, is not broad and linear, not designed, like, for example, Boulevard Haussman, as the objective correlative of patriarchal power; rather, it is narrow, and winding, more suggestive of the feminine principle than the masculine. The street is further connected with feelings rather than the rational spirit when a trip through it is compared to a trip through "the sacred city of the soul" (144). That the street is described as one that "skirted" the back of the Pantheon aligns it linguistically and sexually with the feminine, as does the dark, mysterious atmosphere: "the old buildings on either side rising so high against the blue that the sun never came down lower than the fifth line of windows, and looking up from the pavement was like looking up from the bottom of a well" (144). This is an environment where because everyone lives together, filial, and by extension neighborly, concerns are facts of life. Noel calls on Ettie and her mother, true, but not regularly. He says that the street offers "not even a convenient connecting link" (144). Ettie is far more free than he to move between worlds of art and culture, and she moves readily, on foot, by her own power.

The wild zone of "The Street of the Hyacinth" separates new Rome from old and as such is marginal territory. Luce Irigaray addresses the topic of marginality as it applies to women's liberation movements: "If

I speak of marginality, it is because, first of all, these movements to some extent keep themselves deliberately apart from institutions and from the play of forces in power, and so forth. 'Outside' the already-existing power relations. Sometimes they even reject intervention—including intervention 'from without'—against any institution whatsoever."[17] The margin as creative space for individuals as well as movements is a feminine space overlapping both civilization and the wild, both light and dark. Interestingly, Ettie and her mother live on the fifth floor of their building, on the story that forms the boundary between the dark below and the light above. Ettie's environment serves to suggest her consciousness in the way women's habitations normally serve as metaphors for states of mind in their writing. Like Mademoiselle Reisz in Kate Chopin's *The Awakening,* she is an artist, living in the light above the city; yet at the same time, her street is a margin separating the natural world, where refuse is tossed from windows, from a world where "a certain degree of falsity" is a prized commodity.

The end of the story presents the crisis, the destruction of The Street of the Hyacinth, which forces Ettie to make the decision that Sharon Dean thinks destroys the story's credibility: Ettie changes her mind and decides to marry Noel.[18] The street is to be demolished, as indeed it must if the status quo is to be maintained. For even though Ettie has long ago been forced to abandon her art, her very environment, the name of the street, recalls to her memories of wild zone power, and she grieves, as did Apollo. Her creative space must be appropriated if another generation of masculinized women artists is not to be engendered. Both Ettie and the street experience "a great downfall," as Noel recognizes. For him, a powerful member of the patriarchy, she, in her unwomanly independence and assertiveness, the street itself, and the neighbors are shameful "modern accretions" that should not be permitted "to disfigure longer the magnificent old pagan temple" (182). By appropriating Ettie's shelter, his class forces her capitulation. He then takes verbal control of her, saying: "If you should fall ill, I think that would be the end. I should then take matters into my own hands, and I don't believe you would be able to keep me off. But why should we wait for illness? It is too great a risk" (182).

Since he knows that her brother's death and her mother's illnesses have left her with debts to pay and, as a result, "out almost the whole of every day," Noel's taking advantage of Ettie is figurative rape, as his "I don't believe you would be able to keep me off" suggests. Katharine Winthrop marries John Ford only after being faced with life as a pauper; likewise, Ettie Macks yields only after being faced with the prospect of homelessness for both herself and her mother. The Street of the Hyacinth, the subversive power it and its inhabitants represent, is torn down, leaving the symbol of conventional, patriarchal, institutionalized religion, the solid structure of the Pantheon, standing.

Conventionally, critics have understood "The Street of the Hyacinth" to end happily, the assumption being that the street is a slum—no place for a lady—and that Ettie, having no real talent for art anyway, gets Noel, what she was really after all along. Evidence from the narrative does not, however, support a happily-ever-after reading. First, Ettie likes the street, feels comfortable there; else why would she, when told of its imminent destruction, say, "I presume we can find another like it" (182). In fact, when Noel had first approached her about marrying him, her immediate assumption had been that in the event of such a marriage, they would live in the Street of the Hyacinth. The description of the street as "obstinately narrow and dark as ever" is Noel's, not Ettie's (182). Doubtless, she has accustomed herself to her neighborhood, where the cobbler downstairs bows on meeting his neighbors on the steps in a sign of respect. Ettie's comfort with the narrow, winding street is implied by her dislike of "the broad, new, tiresome piazza Indipendenza" (181), an architectural paean to patriarchal might. Her lamenting the street's capitulation is her only way of grieving the necessity of her own surrender.

Our internalized patriarchal assumption that Ettie's work lacks merit also requires deconstruction. First, the authorities who deem it undeserving are all members of the male-dominated Roman artistic establishment: Noel, Jackson, Bellot, and Salviati. Noel even admits that his motives are selfish rather than generous. And we learn from Ettie and Noel's tour of the Doria that her taste runs quite counter to his: "She gave him a close attention, almost always a comprehension, but seldom agreement." She deems Raphael's double portrait "very ugly," the del Piombo portrait of Andrea Doria "uglier still," the Velasquez "ugliest of all," and the two large Claude Lorraines "rather pretty; but insipid," with no "reality or meaning in them." The Memling he queries her on next "hasn't a redeeming point," she declares (158). Her own work has, we learn from Noel's perspective, "originality," something to be feared: a threat even though her "execution is not much yet" (164). In accepting the judgment of Noel and his cohorts, we too deny faith, falling into the patriarchal trap of assigning value by following conservative, male-dominated criteria. Indeed, we are asked to have faith that Ettie's painting is bad when we are offered no evidence except reaction from a patriarchal establishment that would be seriously threatened by revolutionary work from a woman.

It is indeed possible that Ettie's work derives from her experience on the margins of life, in the Street of the Hyacinth, on the fifth floor where the light juxtaposes with the dark; that her art is a new, wild form of female self-expression. She may work, like her mother, with great splashes of color swearing at each other, playing with dark and light rather than with realistic technique in an effort to create an artificial reality. Woolson, who followed the European art scene, wrote that Miss Macks appears "on the canvas" of Noel's "Roman impressions," a description that calls into account the Impressionist movement in painting. Monet's painting *Impression Sunrise,* the work that launched the Impressionist movement, was done in 1872, and the term *Impressionism,* originally a pejorative description, made its way into the English language in the early 1880s. The movement was reviled by the artistic establishment as having abandoned the tough reality of neoclassicism and the vigorous activity of romanticism as being, perhaps, less masculine, less rigorous than the movements preceding. In any case, Ettie Macks's experience may well have led her to paint in an impressionistic mode, placing colors side by side rather than blending them in an attempt to approximate reality, observing the play of dark and light: a method readily suggested, I would think, by her environment on the Street of the Hyacinth. This self-assertive technique may threaten Noel and his crowd, one of whom defends herself by admitting that she knows "nothing of modern art," in fact, "detest[s] it" (156).

Although I do not want to push this suggestion too far, the possibility exists that Ettie is, in fact, a fine artist whose teachers disapprove of her technique and succeed in discouraging her. We buy into Raymond Noel's conservative values system and lose faith if we believe, like Rayburn S. Moore, that the difference between Ettie Macks and Aaronna Moncrief is that "Ettie Macks has no artistic talent and 'Miss Grief' has; and, in the second place, Ettie finds her fulfillment in a marriage with her mentor, whereas 'Miss Grief' finds hers in her work."[19]

But Ettie and Aaronna and Katharine—and Constance—are all distinctly interesting variations on the theme of the plight of the female artist in the late nineteenth century. In fact, there is no appreciable difference among these Woolson heroines. True, Aaronna dies, but the others are effectively silenced as well. And Ettie is an artist instead of a writer; however, as Ellen Moers notes, painting is "probably the most popular of the mysteries that novelists have always used as substitutes for their own."[20] Termed disfiguring (and often disfigured—consider contemporary portraits of bluestockings) "modern accretions," each of these women is barred, or at least discouraged, from satisfying both artistic and maternal-conjugal drives simultaneously.

Woolson herself chose the artistic route, which necessitated, for her, a life of spinsterhood. Marriage for her meant abandoning art. Coming as she did from a strong nuclear as well as extended family, Woolson's decision to choose a life of art rather than of marriage and motherhood, the option condoned and enforced by the patriarchy, must have been difficult. We see her attempting to rationalize her choice in a letter to a friend in which she remarks: "Family people appear to think that unmarried people are very self-indulgent because they want to amuse themselves. It does not seem to occur to them that they (the married) gave themselves the pleasures which *they* preferred. Let them bear, then, the accompanying cares, and not criticize those who refrained from such ties."[21]

Choosing artistry, for either Woolson or her characters, meant sacrificing the possibility of a life endorsed by a conservative society and relegating gender and sexuality to a near nonexistent role in their lives. Conversely, choosing marriage meant abandoning the opportunity for individual identity. Either choice brings grief to Woolson's protagonists. Their stories are all in their own ways hyacinths signifying the grievous results of suppressed artistry. Sadder yet, however, is the recognition that in the end of "The Street of the Hyacinth" the hyacinth, itself the sign of grief, the commemoration of the beauty and artistry that once was, is demolished, consigning all memory—and faith—to oblivion.

EIGHT • *FOR THE MAJOR:* THE ARTISTRY OF GRIEF

Acknowledged by Woolson to be her own best work, *For the Major* is, like her other artist-heroine narratives, pitched in a minor key. Here, too, the heroine's art violates societal, more specifically patriarchal, expectations. In this novella, however, Woolson presents a twist: the protagonist, Madame Marion Carroll, grande dame of the Farms, her husband's family's estate in the Carolina mountains, is not a dramatist–prose fiction writer like Aaronna Moncrief or a poet like Katharine Winthrop or a painter like Ettie Macks. Rather, she, like Edith Wharton's Lily Bart, exercises her artistry on the canvas of self. Palette in hand, she works to create illusions designed to ensure her own physical survival. She makes herself appear prettier, younger, richer, better bred than she actually is in order to marry well and to live comfortably: her body becomes the narrative. Because her art is more fundamental than that of characters who find artistic expression in paintings, prose, or poetry, languages external to self, it is invested with more risk. When self becomes the artistic creation, the narrative recording it is doubly compelling.

Henry James recognized the powerful nature of the theme of self-artistry, commenting: "The conception of Madame Carroll is highly ingenious and original, and the small stippled portrait has a real fascination. It is the first time that a woman has been represented as painting her face, dyeing her hair, and 'dressing young,' out of tenderness for another: the effort usually has its source in tenderness for herself."[1] In fact, he used the situation in an infrequently read story of his own, "Glasses," written two years after Woolson's death and thirteen years after the publication of *For the Major.* Both works treat the subject of feminine beauty and the theme of the power that attends a pretty face.

In the James piece, a male narrator tells what he thinks is the story of a vain woman who, because she refuses to wear the thick glasses that will mar her breathtaking beauty but save her vision, goes blind. "Her idolatry of her beauty" is her sin, and she pays for it by being forced in the end to marry a rather ugly, unfashionable gentleman.[2] Flora Saunt loses the gamble that her vision will hold out until she has secured a suitable mate: in losing her sight, she loses her control. The narrator usurps her lost power, transforming it into pity. For him, she is more beautiful than ever in her blindness at the opera, acting the role of the sighted beauty, accepting from her box the homage of the crowd, only because her powerlessness ensures his own security. To be sure, James understood the status quo, as his essay on "Modern Women" records: "It is a very dismal truth that the only hope of most women, at the present moment, for a life worth the living, lies in marriage, and marriage with rich men or men likely to become so."[3] And although James may not have the same vested interest in Flora Saunt as the narrator does, in the end both feel pity for her sad plight, thus robbing her of power.

In Woolson's *For the Major,* however, Madame Carroll retains full control even as she loses her beauty. As the novella opens, the reader is introduced to Far Edgerley, a small, isolated Carolina community presided over by the Carrolls, of "the Farms," and to Madame Carroll, who awaits the homecoming of her stepdaughter, Sara, who has been living with Northern relatives for many years. At the end of the opening scene, the narrative voice wonders who is the elder: Madame or Sara.

In the following passage, one of several set in the local Episcopal church, the junior warden traces the Carroll family history. Major Scarborough Carroll had first been married to Sara Witherspoon-Meredith, who bore him two sons, both of whom had died, and Sara, after whose birth the mother passed away. When Sara was only seven years old, the fifty-six-year-old major had married the current Madame Carroll, then a widow named Morris with one little girl. The junior warden assumes that at her marriage "she could not have been then more than twenty one or two; a little fairy-like girl-mother" (271).

Family life at the Farms accommodates Sara to its pattern: Scar, the young son of the major and his second wife, taking his lessons from the major; the family attending church on Sunday and hosting receptions; Sara and Madame calling on other women in the community; the major's senility growing. Frederick Owen, the rector, calls frequently and is received either by one or by both of the Carroll women. Early in August, a stranger—an artist with "unlimited genius" (305), who violates local custom in more ways than one—arrives and disrupts life in the rural community. Because Madame Carroll sanctions his artistry, Louis Dupont is welcomed into society. Neither Sara nor the rector, however, approves of him.

Thus, Owen is shocked when he discovers Sara, of whom he has grown fond, and the despised and apparently dissipated Dupont meeting privately in the woods, and he goes to the Farms to register his concern with Madame Carroll. To protect her stepmother from the charges the rector prepares to level at Dupont, Sara steps in to declare that she is engaged to the artist. As time passes, the musician falls ill, and Sara and Madame Carroll attend him in death at the home of a nearby farmer. Only at his demise does the reader discover that Dupont is really Madame Carroll's son by her first marriage.

Finally, Madame Carroll tells Sara the whole truth about her past. She had been over thirty-five when she had married the major, but because he had so loved the "little blue-eyed, golden-haired girl-mother, unacquainted with the dark side of life, trusting, sweet" (341), Madame Carroll had done her best to preserve the illusion of her youth and innocence. She had told no one, not her daughter Cecilia, not the major, about her cruel husband, Tom Morris, and the son he had taken from her. When Dupont became sick, however, she had told Sara, whose personal money helped him in his last illness. Sara's confessing her engagement to Dupont was designed to divert the rector's attention, thus protecting her stepmother and, in turn, her father. Furthermore, the reader discovers that Dupont's father had not, in fact, drowned in fleeing his wife and the law after killing another man in an argument, meaning that Madame Carroll had married the major while she was still someone else's wife. To legitimate their son and to secure her inheritance as well as to sanctify her commitment to her husband, Madame Carroll arranges to exchange vows with the senile major on Easter Sunday, thus ending the narrative.

The chief issue of the novella is that Madame Carroll uses her prettiness, her blond curls and blue ribbons, to strike a marriage bargain, thus ensuring her own and her young daughter's security. She suffers to maintain that appearance for the major's sake, out of affection and appreciation. Her power, however, lies in her character, not in her artificially maintained beauty, for when the major loses his faculties, Madame Carroll allows Far Edgerley to see her as she is, with graying hair and wrinkled skin.

In the James narrative, however, Flora is powerless: she accepts self-abnegating philosophies of love, art, beauty. The reader is meant to pity her, pity implying a patronizing attitude of those doing the pitying, since they feel themselves advantaged. As Woolson writes in her notebook: "I don't feel so sure about the sympathy of Mrs. B——'s great 'pity.' It seems to me but a way of manifesting her own superiority, and the superiority of every one belonging to her. She is 'so sorry' for Mrs. A—— on account of her children. That means in reality that her own children are to be commended; or if she has no children, then that *she*, as a mother would have done far better than Mrs. A—— has done."[5] Pity, Woolson feels, is a comfortable emotion since it implies power that, in James, belongs to an imagined ideal male reader. Female readers of James are incited to become male readers and to pity James's female characters—at least until Maggie Verver steps onto the scene in *The Golden Bowl* and begins manufacturing her own power and identity.

Madame Carroll, however, is neither victimized nor left impotent at the end of the narrative. She successfully asserts selfhood, having acquired the authority that attends its discovery in choosing both to write the fiction of her life and to reveal its made-up character. Not a woman to be pitied despite the history of her life, which has included a loveless marriage, the presumed death of a son and the sure death of a daughter, poverty, and the mental anguish attending such hardship, Marion Carroll is an essential, creative spirit and the only successful female artist in Woolson's canon. Although her art is actually artifice exercised on her own body, her talent for making herself appear younger than she really is has provided her with the material security and loving respect she had long lacked.

Her strength has been suggested by several commentators who read *For the Major* as an allegory of the demise of the domestic heroine. Ann Douglas Wood writes that the femininity that Marion Carroll affects is just a "sentimental façade," "both a luxury given the more pressing concerns of life with which Madame Carroll is all too familiar, and a painful necessity, given the needs of men to have women appear what they think they should be."[6] Sybil B. Weir concurs that sentimental ideals of womanhood and community are overturned in Woolson's novella by exposing their fraudulent nature through the exemplary character of Madame Carroll, who appears to be "the little woman." Both critics suggest the Madame Carroll is "imprisoned by the appurtenances of the sentimental heroine," who already had to cope with "mistreatment, unfairness, disadvantage, and powerlessness."[7] For Woolson, a writer of this postsentimental narrative that plays off the conventions of its predecessors, the issues are essentially the same; however, the emphasis has changed from the heroine's learning to live with a lack of control to her acquiring and maintaining power.

The setting of the story, its physical situation as well as its moment in history, suggests how power operates in the feminist politics of *For the Major.* For example, the town's pastoral locale and consequent purposeful rejection of anything new or "commercial" (outside *The Saturday Review*) imply its conservative refusal to move with the times. Coupled with the Southern setting, the date, 1868, three years after the Confederate surrender at Appomattox, suggests a loss of potency, a forfeiture of power, validated by the detail concerning the "high-hung" equipage, once belonging to the Sea Island Carrolls, the Carrolls of the patriarchal plantation culture, but now stabled at the domestic Farms: "This was as well. The Sea Island Carrolls had no longer any use for a carriage. They had not even mules to draw it, and, as they lived all the year round now upon one of their sea islands, whose only road through the waste of old cotton fields was most of the time overflowed, they had nothing to draw it upon" (260).

The most interesting aspect of the setting, however, seems to be that the very landscape that suggests the male impotence of King Cotton points simultaneously to a powerful female fecundity. Ellen Moers has remarked that "the very names that women writers have given to their personal landscapes—indeed, have imposed on their homeland through sheer force of language—are sexually suggestive."[8] *For the Major* takes place in a space that is unquestionably feminine. Far Edgerley is situated six hundred feet above Edgerley on the eastern flank of Chillawassee Mountain opposite the Black Range and in view of Lonely Mountain. Once up Chillawassee, one has to cross "the little bridge over the brook which crossed what was called Carroll Lane, the grassy avenue which led from Edgerley Street up the long knoll to Carroll Farms" (260). Up the "flank" of the mountain, sheltered by others—the Black and the Lonely—surrounded by grass, Carroll Farms, Marion Carroll's personal space, suggests the womb: dark, distant, difficult to reach, but pleasurable and safe once realized.

In many ways, Woolson's depiction of the Farms is allied with the image of the house in both sentimental and local color fiction. Ann Douglas Wood explains: "In the fiction of the sentimentalists, the home was an emblem of what they liked to call female 'influence.' . . . it was a symbol of their own inner space, into whose rich and warm atmosphere they . . . invited the privileged male, exhausted from his debilitating conflict with the competitive world."[9] On the contrary, Wood continues, in local color fiction, the house may be "barren, and even poisonous," in any case, life-destroying rather than life-enhancing, "a source of death rather than life."[10] Marion Carroll's private space cannot be explained quite so easily, for it nurtures, following the sentimental pattern, as well as stunts growth, following Wood's local color pattern. We can note this double capacity in Madame Carroll's relationship to the several characters in the story: she is full of love in her nursing of her husband, yet she hates the rector for his admission of distrust of the artistic stranger; she goes out of her way to promote the stranger, who turns out to be her son by her first marriage, yet she responds coolly toward her son by the major, a sickly, dwarfish child, perhaps from a fear of growing close then losing him to death. Neither a true angel of the house nor an Old Woman Magoun, Marion Carroll exists on the margin, on the threshold of these two traditions, as her setting, on the edge of civilization, suggests.[11]

The very name of her residence, Far Edgerley, implies Madame Carroll's marginality, for she lives at the far edge not only of civilization but also of time and gender, in a womb, on the margin, in a woman's territory if ever there was one. As we expect, Far Edgerley supports no—nor has ever had any need for—businesses such as factories, sawmills, or stage lines, all identified with the patriarchy in their linear as well as commercial design. From the perspective of the village inhabitants, mostly women with names like Corinna (reminiscent of Mme de Staël) and Honoria, women who, despite their age, outshine the weak, small-voiced, and elderly men in the village, Far Edgerley is the center of the universe. The inhabitants do not see themselves as far from Edgerley: "It was 'far,' if you pleased—far from cities, far from traffic, from Babylon, from Zanzibar, from the Pole—but it was not 'far' from Edgerley. Rather was Edgerley far from it, and—long may she keep so!" (259).

How, we might ask, can Far Edgerley be on the edge yet in the center? Description appears to defy reason until we realize that in *For the Major,* a narrative of female accumulation and exercise of power, the efficacy of the patriarchy—its power of naming, its entire system of signification—is called into question by a female power structure suggested as a replacement. On the Farms, in the womblike shelter of the mountains, Marion Carroll exists in a kind of Garden of Eden, where she sets schedules, names names, and generally runs the show. She becomes the female artist par excellence, the goddess figure.

Henry James understood the incongruent nature of Marion Carroll as an artist-heroine when he wrote in his *Partial Portraits* sketch of Woolson that she had "done nothing of a neater execution than this fanciful figure of the little ringletted, white-frocked, falsely juvenile lady, who has the toilet table of an actress and the conscience of a Puritan."[12] In that assessment he remarks the obvious double irony of the narrative. For though Madame Carroll's painting herself is a fiction, her motive is honorable: not only is she not what she appears to be, but also the motive, normally vanity, a vice to be avoided, in this narrative is love, a motive to be praised. I submit, however, that more than irony is at stake here: that Woolson attempts to undermine the whole patriarchal sign system that designates the Carrolls' Edgerley "Far" and the Farms' mistress a domestic angel. The subverting of that system has ramifications for gender, for fiction, and for the potentiality of female artistry in a postlapsarian, patriarchally organized world.

Madame Carroll is, like her womblike, Edenic setting, full of mystery and potential for power and artistry, as her typical apparel abundantly illustrates. Indeed, the white dress is appropriate for the maintenance of the illusion of youth she wishes to reinforce; however, as a signifier of freshness, of innocence, the dress lies: as a sign, it is undone. The white dress iconography of purity is further subverted when we discover that Madame Carroll has kept the tale of one child's birth a complete secret, further impugning her "purity" of heart. But Madame Carroll's white apparel does more than point up her scheme to keep the major in the dark about her past and her true age. It also works to suggest the mysterious potentiality of her selfhood in the same way that Emily Dickinson's power manifests itself in her white garb.

Gilbert and Gubar's analysis of Emily Dickinson's penchant for dressing in white impinges on Madame Carroll's character. They explain: "For white, in Dickinson's poetry, frequently represents both the energy (the white heat) of Romantic creativity, and the loneliness (the polar cold) of the renunciation or tribulation Romantic creativity may demand, both the white radiance of eternity—or Revelation—and the white terror of a shroud."[13] The white dress, in its absence of color, they continue, "is a blank page that asks to be written on," implying "that she exists only and completely for the man who will remove it."[14] Yet, they continue, it also suggests the refusal of the assumed invitation to violate her virginity.[15] For the white gown of the lady also signals cold, hard power. White, in other words, only pretends to mirror man's desire, only playacts a reflective stance. In fact, it asserts in its absence of color, the power residing in the containment of all color, all creativity. For the junior warden, Madame Carroll in her white gown may resemble "a Hebe," the youthful cupbearer to the gods, but we know that, in fact, she orchestrates her existence so that the town brings things to her, not vice versa.

When Madame Carroll is not in white, signaling her virginal character, she is often in blue, implying the mystery and potentiality of an iconography older than the Victorians'. For in traditional Christian iconography, the Virgin Mary is, more often than not, pictured wearing blue, the color Marion Carroll dons after the death of her first begotten son. In her guise as Mary, Marion is the embodiment of the Eternal Feminine, the fundamental mother, affiliated, attached, dependent: the Eve in the garden of the Farms. Indeed, all of the villagers recognize her specialness, praising her in terms reminiscent of Mariolatry. As the junior warden effuses: "She is—a domestic angel, yet a very muse in culture; one of the loveliest women, one of the most engaging, upon my word, that ever walked the face of this earth, and honored it with her tread" (271). She is quite literally the inheritor of her mother's name, Mary Foster, who defines nurturance, caring as she does for every need, both physical and spiritual, of both children and husband. Moreover, she cares deeply for her community, as her explanation of her social duties makes clear. For when her stepdaughter, Sara, suggests the possibility of dropping fictitious customs, Marion Carroll responds: "If we should drop them . . . Far Edgerley, socially speaking, would disappear. It would become a miscellaneous hamlet upon a mountain top, like any other. It would dissolve into its component parts, which are, as you know, but ciphers; we, of the Farms, hold them together, and give them whatever importance they possess" (265).

Her gender presents Marion with the opportunity for the broadest kind of artistic production, the bearing of children, and her role as mother offers her the motive to create a fictitious text of self. First, in her marriage to Tom Morris, Marion is able to create two other narrative voices, one that we hear and another that we don't, in the persons of Cecilia, a sickly baby whose name is borrowed from the patron saint of music, and Julian, her firstborn son. It is he who is the more conventional artist in the tale. Deemed a genius and an original, he assaults Far Edgerley's sense of propriety by wearing "low shoes with red silk stockings above them, and a red silk handkerchief to match the stocking peeping from the breast pocket of the coat; a cream-colored umbrella lined with red silk; a quantity of cream-colored gauze wound round a straw hat" (306). A long loop of red ribbon is attached to his guitar so that he may sling it over his shoulder. Red, then, the color of Isis and a suggestion of female creative potential, and also the color of blood, is associated with Julian, the son of Marion, in the same way that Virgin white and Marian blue are associated with the mother. Undoubtedly, Woolson is working from a Mary-Jesus model in her creation of the Marion-Julian relationship, as exemplified in the pietà tableau of Madame Carroll's tending her dying son.

Her finest creation, Julian takes after his mother, almost subsuming the female creative sense. His songs, for example, are brief, unsustained, like the women's local color writing of the period; and he sings in a high-pitched voice, "a tenor, not powerful, but deliciously, sensuously sweet," like a woman's, we might imagine (309). Moreover, he sings songs of oppressed peoples—"the wild, soft, plaintive cadences of the Indian women of tribes long gone towards the setting sun, of the first African slaves poling their flatboats along the Southern rivers" (309). His penchant for love songs and flower gardens and his erratic, fantastic disposition further associate him more with the traditional feminine personality than with the masculine of the Victorian strong, silent school. As an artist, however, he is permitted to bridge that gender gap, as the name he takes after moving to the islands—Dupont—insists. The product of female creativity, he reproduces his mother's desire for self-expression in the same way that Ettie Macks does her mother's and Avis Dobell does hers. His feminine traits qualify his desire for affiliation, yet his gender permits his genius and originality. Just as the world is not ready for the offspring of other women artists, however, the conservative community of Far Edgerley is not prepared to accept Louis-Julian's walking the boundaries of gender. He and his artistry must exit the scene.

Marion Carroll's greatest grief in a narrative replete with it (the word *grief* appears ten times) occurs as a result of burying her best creation, of never, in fact, being able to recognize their relationship, of having to deny the fruit of her womb. Early in the story the junior warden calls Madame Carroll "a veritable hyacinth" (298) because of the simple lavender muslin she wears: he has no idea how appropriate the emblematic reference is to designate the grief of a creator whose best work must be unacknowledged.

If she is unable to declare her artistry as it manifests itself in her son, however, Marion Carroll finally reveals the high art of her fiction of self, to the profound amazement of both her stepdaughter and the village. Marion Carroll had made herself into a fictional text, calculated and designed to ensure both her own and her daughter's survival. To Sara she narrates the tale of her years of struggle, which prompted the then Marion Morris to create the first layer of her fictional self:

> I was alone in the world with my delicate little girl, who needed so much that I could not give—luxuries, constant care, the best advice. I had strained every nerve, made use of all my poor little knowledge and my trifling accomplishments; I had worked as hard as I possibly could; and the result of all my efforts was that I had barely succeeded in getting our bread from day to day, with nothing laid up for the future, and the end of my small strength near at hand. For I was not fitted for that kind of struggle, and I knew that I was not. I could work and plan and accomplish, and even, I believed, successfully, but only when sheltered—sheltered in a home, no matter how plain, protected from actual contact with the crowd. . . . What were my small plans, which always concerned themselves with the delicate little things and details, in the great pushing struggle for bread? It was when I was fully realizing the hopelessness of all my efforts, when the future was at its blackest, and I could not look at Cecilia without danger of tears—for they had told me that something might be done for her during the next year—for her poor spine—and I had not the money to pay for it—it was then that your father's love came to me like a gift straight down from heaven. (342–343)

As Wood and Weir imply, this is a version of the conventional fiction of the sentimental heroine, who, bereft of family and sustenance, must exist by her wits.[16]

This fictional self, like other fictions, elicits an interpretive critical fiction, as much an invention as the work that prompts it. The major, Marion tells Sara, no longer distinguishes fiction from facts. "What were once surmises he now thinks facts, and he fully believes in them. He has constructed a sort of history, and has woven in all sorts of imaginary theories in the most curious way. For instance, he thinks that my mother was one of a family well known in New York—so they tell me, at least. . . . My mother was plain Mary Foster, from Chester, Vermont, or its neighborhood, a farmer's daughter.[17] In the same way he has built up a belief that my father was an Episcopal clergyman, and that he was educated in England. My father was a Baptist missionary; he was a man of fair education (he educated me), but he was never in England in his life" (346–347).

In this way Marion Carroll directs development of her fiction of self, layer by layer, the first layer being the sentimental drama, the next being her physical fiction of doll's face and curls, supplemented by her encompassing the major's own reader-response interpretation of her history. She, too, adopts the fictional (as Sara Carroll realizes) conventions appropriate to the lady of the manor: the assumption of the name of the patriarch, the attendance at church services, the elaborate receptions. Finally Marion Carroll is quite another being entirely from Marion Morris. She is a fiction whose layered text has kept her safe and warm.

How she has managed this fictional tour de force is the magic of the narrative of *For the Major,* for Marion Carroll is able to construct her life-sustaining façade by manipulation of signs. She admits to being clever, but no one, even when she reveals the artifice of her physical beauty, recognizes that in her subversion of societal codes, she has managed not only to provide for her own physical security, but also to appropriate the power of language—and of art—for herself. Luce Irigaray's commentary in "The Power of Discourse and the Subordination of the Feminine" offers provocative ramifications for a reading of *For The Major:*

> There is, in an initial phase, perhaps only one "path," the one historically assigned to the feminine: that of *mimicry.* One must assume the feminine role deliberately. Which means already to convert a form of subordination into an affirmation, and thus to begin to thwart it. . . .

> To play with mimesis is thus, for a woman, to try to recover the place of her exploitation by discourse, without allowing herself to be simply reduced to it. It means to resubmit herself—inasmuch as she is on the side of the "perceptible," of "matter"—to "ideas," in particular to ideas about herself, that are elaborated in/by a masculine logic, but so as to make "visible," by an effect of playful repetition, what was supposed to remain invisible: the cover-up of a possible operation of the feminine in language.[18]

Indeed, Madame Carroll is the mirror image, *Une Mère de Glace* (a mirror mother, whom Irigaray discusses elsewhere),[19] of the major's idea of youthful charm and femininity. But her power resides in her recognition that she is able to control her specular nature. To be sure, in her reflective white apparel, she mirrors patriarchal expectation, but in so doing, subverts the power base. In recognizing the artificiality of the sign-signifier relationship (here neither dressing in frills nor wearing curls effectively translates to actual youth), Madame Carroll threatens the coherence of the discourse pursued by the major in educating Scar.

Her artistry of self resides in the manipulation of signs whose meaning the patriarchal culture takes for granted, such as the language and the physical features connoting female attractiveness and desirability. We may examine, for example, the frequent assertions of Madame Carroll's tiny stature. As Ellen Moers writes, "Littleness as a physical fact, though only a relative one, is inescapably associated with the female body, and as long as writers describe women they will all make use of the diminutive in language and the miniature in imagery."[20] Littleness in patriarchal terms has signaled youth, triviality, and powerlessness. Whenever this attribute has been used for men, it has feminized them or rendered them impotent in some way, as in Dickens's Tiny Tim or Little Dorritt. Yet the signifier does not accurately reflect the signified in the case of Madame Carroll: the sign lies. For, in fact, she is old and powerful, though not following a patriarchal pattern: her age and power, ironically disguised as youth and weakness, are used to create and maintain continuity and filiation rather than to declare independence and ownership. Her behind-the-scenes manipulations have made her a force to be reckoned with. In this way, we may recognize that Madame Carroll also manipulates her apparel and her grooming to elicit signs that lie. Her golden hair, for example, a conventionalized fairy-tale sign of youth and beauty, is artificially colored. Likewise her white dress lies: not only is she not young and virginal, but also she is not the mirror of Carroll nature. Rather, she creates it.

The sweep of her power encompasses the entire village, and she organizes the lives of the townspeople as well as that of her husband. For example, when she begins to hold her receptions at night, the sign tells the community that Madame Carroll has decided to inject the custom with additional festivity and gravity. In fact, however, she is adjusting the time so that the daylight will not reveal her secrets. She orchestrates the major's appearances both at church and at the receptions in an effort to create the "all's well" sign and thus to guarantee the security of the parish. The reader knows, of course, that the major must prepare for each appearance by extensive rest. In other words, all is not well.

Madame Carroll is such a successful user of language because she has no illusions about inherent meaning, about the patriarchally designated integrity of the sign. Without custom, a sign system designed to invest empty signifieds with meaning, Far Edgerley "would dissolve into its component parts, which are, as you know, but ciphers; we, of the Farms, hold them together, and give them whatever importance they possess," Madame Carroll explains. Similarly, given the dresses of the Greer sisters, one may pretend that their custom of altering their supplementary trim gives the dresses new meaning; however, they remain "the same green poplins" (263), ciphers in themselves.

Traces of never-ending relationships between one dress and another ("Miss Corinna Rendlesham, too, and her sisters have accomplished wonders with different combinations of narrow black velvet ribbon and fringe on their black silks—so much so, indeed, that the material is now quite riddled with the old lines of needle-holes where trimmings formerly ran" [263]), between mother and child, bind Far Edgerley together, rather than any comprehensive logocentric sign system. Here the word of the father no longer operates.

That Word had been incarnate in the pre–Civil War Southern civilization, where cotton was king and men worked the land until it would no longer bear fruit. During that time the Carroll family had owned cotton plantations on the Carolina Sea Islands. The world of the Old South, a civilization that abided by, as Woolson saw it, a charming but outmoded chivalric code, was one whose time had passed. Yet, the major insists on teaching his son its precepts, its language:

> "Good-Blood-can-not-lie. . . .
>
> "A brave father makes a brave son. . . .
>
> "The-knights-are-dust.—Their-good-swords-rust.—Their-souls-are-with-the-saints-we-trust." (280)

(The validity of this last maxim, of course, foreshadows the end of the narrative and asserts further that *For the Major* deconstructs the logocentric universe.) These codes, however, of chivalry and lineage have lost significance in the encroaching commercial world to which Louis Dupont is a bridge. Their signs no longer signify. In years past, the code of the major's demeanor would have signaled him a modern knight in shining armor: "He was a handsome, soldierly-looking man, tall, broad-shouldered, with noble bearing, and bold, well-cut features. He was dressed in black, with broad, stiff, freshly starched white cuffs, and a high standing collar, round which was folded a black silk cravat that when opened was three-quarters of a yard square. His thin gray hair, moustache, and imperial were cut after the fashion affected by the senior officers of the old army—the army before the war" (281). The war, or as the junior warden calls it "Our Sacred Cause," lost, the signs on which the civilization had been built lose currency and meaning: finally they do not tell the truth about the present. For example, Major Carroll has thought his second wife to have come from fine breeding, but here "good blood" does, in fact, lie. Similarly, although the major is believed to have behaved bravely in wartime, his son by Madame Carroll is small and weak. A brave father does not necessarily make a brave son.

Significance subverted, the logocentric authority of the father disappears. His word, his identity, his son, who possesses his very name—is, in fact, but a scar: a trace memory of what was. In this case Scar, a small, weak child, is all that remains of patriarchal authority at the end of *For the Major:* The old man murmurs softly to himself in the last line of the novella, "Yes, certainly I remember; little Scar" (367).

The old man's loss of wits and vision reiterates his loss of linguistic command and the breakdown of power based on patriarchal possession of the word. Once the authority of the father has been dismantled, the usurper, Madame Carroll, can take over. She appropriates the language of the wedding vows, at the time essentially a writ by which the male took possession of the female body, by repeating the rector's words for her husband and changes the gender stereotypes written into the language. As he worries about his hair, she takes control of the ceremony. In the end, she is the only one able to comprehend his unclear speech.

The patriarchy is replaced by matriarchal order, which is ensured by the marriage ceremony at the end. (Although the wedding may seem only a sentimental gesture by Madame Carroll, she must renew her vows [since technically she had still been married to Tom Morris when she had first taken them] in order to inherit her husband's goods, thus guaranteeing her continued security and safety.) Throughout the narrative Madame Carroll has asserted her power by her artful management of fictions for her own purposes. She has recognized how the language of custom works in maintaining a close community, filiation being a value demonstrated by Nancy Chodorow and others to be particularly important to women.[21] Similarly, she has manipulated the language of sentimental beauty, fashioning herself into an art object, even a fetish or a commodity, turning herself into a fictional text—for purposes of her own and her daughter's survival.

All along, of course, she has been the artist, recognizing fully how language operates. As the text reveals: "But a presence is more than an absence. Absent as were all signs of age in Madame Carroll, as present were all signs of youth in the daughter who had just arrived" (264). Presence is, as some contemporary theorists might explain, a supplemented absence, like the fictitious presence of the apparently youthful lady of the Farms. The absence of any "sign of age"—wrinkles, gray hair, aging skin—is supplemented by "the veil of curls and the close ruffles of the dress, the latter falling over the hands almost to the knuckles. There was really nothing of the actual woman to be seen save a narrow, curl-shaded portion of forehead and cheek, two eyes, a little nose and mouth, and the small fingers; that was all" (264). Stripped of supplements when she reveals her artistry, she appears in a black dress. No longer apparently young, the face now reflects a metaphor of matriarchal order: "a network of minute wrinkles" (355).

" 'Men,' " she says at one point, " 'are dull. . . . They have to have everything explained to them' " (361). Perhaps that is because their vested interest in the integrity of the sign betrays their desires for connection at the expense of reality. It takes a woman of the stuff of Madame Carroll or Sara Carroll, as we shall see, to discern the discrepancy between signifier and signified. As Marion Carroll tells Sara of her artist-son's reappearance at Far Edgerley, " 'That watch chain and ring he had when he came back—they were only gilt' " (345).

In a patriarchal logocentric culture, the word of the father is law and law is power. In a deconstructed patriarchal culture, such as the one operating at Far Edgerley, in the female territory of the womblike state, the word of the mother is art and art is power. The laws of blood, knights, and name are replaced with transcendent and all-encompassing mother love and sacrifice, which are supplemented into existence by an artistry of grief. In other words, Madame Carroll gains her power through the artistry of her fiction of self: a narrative necessitated by the grief of her past life of poverty as well as of her present life of artifice created to shield her husband from his debilitation.

Several traditions of goddess worship and mythology support Marion Carroll's artistic power. On one interpretive level, she is a Juno figure, Juno being the wife of Jupiter, king of the gods, and the mother of Vulcan, the celestial artist separated from his mother in his youth. Juno, or Hera, had, in ancient Arcadia, three forms: maiden, fulfilled woman, and woman of sorrows. Certainly, Madame Carroll is a narrative reworking of this figure in her roles as virginal consort to the major, artful negotiator of community custom, and suffering wife and mourning mother. She also retells the Demeter-Kore myth, in which Demeter is the mourning mother, a weaver, the goddess of the seasons, especially the rebirth of spring, and Kore the virgin daughter.[22] In some versions of the story, the two are considered an unfolding of the same being. Indeed, Madame Carroll weaves the fiction that enables her to dress in the role of the virginal daughter while being, in fact, the mother mourning her dead child. Moreover, like Demeter, she organizes the seasonal system: her narrative begins in May, in the spring; her son is taken from her in October, near the beginning of the winter; and he, a type of Jesus, is figuratively restored to her at the end of the narrative, on Easter, the feast of the Resurrection. This movement in *For the Major* from spring to spring follows the seasonal cycle of the Demeter-Kore myth, which aligns mother love with artistic production (the weaving of the narrative) and reproduction (the continuation of the community's agrarian economy).

But Madame Carroll is not the only Kore figure in *For the Major:* her stepdaughter Sara will inherit her power. The lines of inheritance, thus, are not patriarchal: the word of the father does not enter into this woman's history since Marion and Sara are not related by blood. As the reader is reminded, Sara is a "Witherspoon-Meredith." Yet she learns matriarchal artistry of narrative and of organization from her father's wife, this an artistry elicited by grief. For example, when she is pressured by the rector to answer for having secretly met Dupont, Sara invents the fiction of her engagement to put him off. Later, she is her stepmother's go-between when Dupont returns to Far Edgerley to die. The first fiction she invents in the spirit of self-sacrifice, as Marion Carroll recognizes. She tells the major's daughter: "The sacrifice you then made in lowering yourself by your own act in his eyes was as great a one as a woman can make" (349).

By the end of the novella, Sara has come into power through following the example of Marion Carroll's artistry. The power of the next generation does not belong to her small, sickly half brother, Scar, who, despite replicating half of Madame Carroll's genes, carries the name of the father. In fact, a case could be made for Scar's imminent death: not only does he not grow, but also his flaxen hair looks like an angel's halo, and he is described as "sitting on a little tombstone in the sunshine" (329). (It is well to note that Madame Carroll's other two children, each puny and sickly, offspring of the oppressed Marion Morris, are already imagined as angels in heaven.) Rather, the power of the future belongs to Sara, who has been taught by her stepmother to appropriate language, fiction, and art. At the end, she is the one to subvert the male sign of lock and key, turning the key in the door of the Farms and so locking it herself (365). She recognizes the artistry of grief that devolves on women, telling Owen, "We suffer more than you do, always" (364). The world of feeling suggested by this remark is "beyond his ken" (365). Finally, Sara is the one who goes to the window prior to the marriage ceremony to break off a spray of apple blossom for her father's buttonhole. She has seized the initiative, the female symbol of potentiality, of fruit to come.

As Luce Irigaray comments, "Engendering the real is the father's task, engendering the fictive is the task of the mother—that 'receptacle' for turning out more or less good copies of reality. Property, ownership, and self-definition are the attributes of the father's production. They define the work of the father 'as such.' To be. To own."[23] In *For the Major* Marion Carroll, the mother, is seen engendering the fictive so masterfully that the results of the father's engendering become little more than a sentimental scar, a trace of lost power. The mother's engendered fiction, however, becomes the artistry of self and of the narrative to which Woolson's name, the name of the mother, is attached. *For the Major* is a fiction created through the commerce of woman and grief. That the artistry of grief is the only possibility offered by a woman's landscape is the lesson Sara Carroll, heir to her stepmother's art, learns. The potential female artist, she comes to understand that she cannot transform from Kore to Demeter, from virgin to mother-weaver-artist, without requisite suffering and self-sacrifice, which become the continually deferred, matriarchal "signs" of female artistry—the authentic word of the mother.

Madame Carroll is an existential artist unlike any of Woolson's other artist-heroines: Miss Elisabetha, Felipa and Catherine, Aaronna Moncrief, Katharine Winthrop, and Ethelinda Faith Macks. Their artistic expressions of self are destined for oblivion because they attempt to seize the patriarchal power of the baton, brush, or pen in a male-dominated world. Inevitably, they suffer the grief of artistry, the abuse of their talents by a fraternity unprepared to admit women to their ranks. Men permit them, however, what they consider the unthreatening womanly attributes—love and self-sacrifice—nonauthoritative traits that, unlike conscious artistic activity, do not presume the power of the patriarchy. Yet, these qualities, generated by the word of the mother, are unremittingly powerful. They undermine the integrity of the logocentric sign and replace it with a different female artistry: the artistry of grief. In that gendered genre, Madame Carroll is an artist indeed.

CONCLUSION

As evidenced by her artist-heroines, Constance Fenimore Woolson felt that for the men controlling her culture's power structure—and its institutionalized mentorship and reward system—the only arena for the exercise and perfection of female artistry was the traditional domestic sphere. Although women would continue to be praised for their genius of love and self-sacrifice, they would not for some time be permitted entry into the world's highest artistic circles. Such was inevitable, Woolson concluded, because social and political power rested in the hands of men, as "'Miss Grief'" so thoroughly demonstrates. Artistic women, like Katharine Winthrop and Ettie Macks, would be forced either to abandon their forms of expression, in favor of secure positions as wives, or to turn their artistic urges to domestic expression of the grief of their lives as unequals in the world. The other choice open to these women was the life of art and its attending spinsterhood, the option Woolson herself elected.

During the last years of her life, when she was under contract to produce serial novels, a form she detested, Woolson returned again and again to the short story genre and to the theme of female artistry. To her heroines, she offers the mutually exclusive possibilities she had rehearsed in earlier works: the artistry of suffering and self-sacrificial love, marriage and the abandonment of formal art, or art and spinsterhood.

Originally written in 1880, "At the Château of Corinne," was not actually published until 1887. Perhaps in 1880, after her mother's death and the publication of "'Miss Grief,'" thinking about another failed artist was simply too painful for Woolson, and she shelved the narrative. The story, if not its underlying theme of female artistry sacrificed to the institutions of publishing or marriage, lay dormant for seven years, until Woolson resurrected it from her files on hearing once again the nostalgic lines from Ronsard that she quotes in the fiction. That the story should have been resurrected at all demonstrates the constancy of the artist-heroine theme for Woolson. Moreover, the short history of its again coming to light suggests that by 1887 Woolson thought female literary artistry like Katharine Winthrop's a nostalgic fantasy. The fate of a woman artist valuing security above all else is the silence of a marriage dominated by a pragmatic patriarch like John Ford.

A little more than a year after "At the Château of Corinne" finally appeared, Woolson published "The Front Yard" in the December 1888 issue of *Harper's New Monthly Magazine.* Critics have agreed that this narrative, reprinted posthumously in 1895 as the title story in *The Front Yard and Other Italian Stories,* is one of her best efforts. In her own day, readers focused on the local color aspects of the tale, which features dialectal speech and the counterpoint between colorful Italian characters and Prudence Wilkin, a New England exile. As the commentator in *The Critic* for 28 December 1895 wrote: "The story is a brilliant piece of genre-painting executed by an artist who understood her subject to the heart."[2] More recently, however, readers have centered on the character of Prudence Wilkin, whom they praise as a domestic saint, self-renunciatory in the finest fashion. As Rayburn S. Moore remarks, "Prudence's notions of honor and duty may appear quixotic to some, but they are basic to her character and so consistently maintained that even the reader who is unwilling to suspend his disbelief is bound to admit that such a nature is possible or, if not, run the risk, as James says . . . 'of denying that a woman *may* look at life from a high point of view.'"[3]

In the context of Woolson's other short fiction, Prudence is another version of Miss Elisabetha and Marion Carroll, who, by sacrificing herself to her family, turns her narrative into art. Prudence's sacrifice, however, is not that of self to a generalized and all-consuming love of family. Her sacrifice is very specific: it is that New England art of domestic landscaping, which translates into identity, respectability, and pride. At the age of forty-five, Prudence Wilkin, a traveling companion to an aged, wealthy cousin, had been captivated by an Italian Romeo, who married the naive New England spinster and conned her out of her savings. Moreover, he had told her that he was unattached when, in fact, he lived with his first wife's mother, uncle, and eight children. Then, after only a year of marriage, he had died, leaving his American wife an exile in Italy. For sixteen years after her husband's death, Prudence works like a pack animal to provide for his family. In fact, when we first see her, she has strapped to her back an enormous basket for hauling goods to market. Since her marriage, she has labored to feed and clothe the family, planning for the day when the children would be grown and she could spend some of her hard-earned funds to tear down the small, ancient, windowless stone building across from the house, a symbol of her bondage: "Bars guarded the entrance; it was impossible to see what was within. But the woman knew without seeing; she always knew. It had been a cow; it had been goats; it had been pigs, and then goats again; for the past two years it had been pigs steadily—always pigs" (185). Prudence's plan is to earn enough money by additional scrimping and saving to level the shed and replace it with a real American front yard, for Prudence an emblem of American domestic—and artistic—virtue. She explains her plan to her slow-witted stepdaughter:

> "I shall have to make the front walk all over. . . . And here'll be the gate, down here—a swing one. And the path will go from here straight up to the door. Then the fence will go along here—palings, you know, painted white; a good clean American white, with none of these yellows in it, you may depend. And over there—and there—along the sides, the fence will be just plain boards, notched at the top; the currant bushes will run along there. In the middle, here—and here—will be the big flowerin' shrubs. And then the little flower beds bordered with box." (212)

Her other selfish stepchildren, however, convince the self-sacrificing Prudence to part with her front yard fund bit by bit for their own needs. Finally, one of them, Giovanni, steals the box to pay a gambling debt. The art of Prudence Wilkin's life is sacrificed to the *will* of her *kin*. Her dream of a front yard, an architectural feature that, she feels, will express her true self within a foreign landscape, is finally accomplished by deae ex machinā: three American women visiting Assisi to sketch and to read make Prudence's dream a reality. Although her Italian husband had robbed her of her freedom and her stepson Giovanni of her nest egg, the American women tourists, representing the cultural values of art, albeit patriarchally institutionalized art, set Prudence free.

Others of Woolson's heroines do not sacrifice their art either to family or to lovers. Instead, by remaining spinsters, they may carry on in that wild zone outside the pale of the community, populated by unmarried women. Traditionally viewed as witches—and worse—spinsters are expected to exhibit eccentricities because they live without a regulating male influence. Because of their marital status, they spin the fabric of narratives, of spells, despite the interdiction of society at large. The spinster becomes Woolson's most important incarnation of the artist heroine in "'Miss Grief.'" She is also Woolson's last incarnation of the female artist in "In Sloane Street" (1892), one of the final short narratives Woolson would write.[4]

"In Sloane Street" offers a prophetic vision of the fate of all literary artistry in the upcoming new century, where selfishness overrides art on the domestic as well as the literary front. Neither women's artistry of sacrifice and self-denial, such as we have seen in "Miss Elisabetha," *For the Major*, and "The Front Yard," nor formal female artistic endeavor in painting, music, or literature, as we have seen in "Felipa," "'Miss Grief,'" "At the Château of Corinne," or "The Street of the Hyacinth," is even attempted. As Philip Moore, the head of the family in the story, self-righteously announces, "Women can't write. And they ought not to try" (474). When Gertrude Remington, the artist figure in the narrative, objects, Philip responds, "*You* need not be troubled, you have never tried. And I'm thankful you haven't. It would be insupportable to me to have any of my personal friends among that band" (474). Gertrude admits that she has never attempted anything, that her "ambition is all for other people" (474). She maintains, however, an artistic sensibility, reading, writing (if not fiction then diaries), and finding art everywhere, including in the commercial announcements, which she views as poetic. She notes that each of the short lines begins "with a capital letter like a poem": "'Wool is weaker. / Leather is slow. / Hides are easy. / Rice is low'" (474).

Gertrude is, in fact, in many ways, a thinly disguised self-portrait. A spinster, Gertrude Remington, like Woolson herself, makes a pilgrimage to George Eliot's grave in Highgate, yearns nostalgically for the Florida climate and landscape, and reads Louisa May Alcott, Marie Bashkirtseff, and Jules LeMaitre. Amy Moore, Philip's wife, calls her Philip's "chief incense burner" (474), nearly echoing Woolson's own confession that she is Henry James's "admiring aunt."[5] Like Woolson (and Miss Elisabetha), Gertrude Remington prefers tailored clothes to loungewear of the sort Cécile Kernadi wears, which Amy Moore insists would make Gertrude appear "more cozy." Moreover, both Remington and Woolson prefer analytical novels, novels that their writers and publishers take seriously. Writing is, for them, after all, a serious business. Gertrude Remington's soul mate is Philip Moore, a childhood friend, a writer who, also like Woolson, does not produce prodigiously. (Woolson, for one, worried that she wrote so very slowly.) Further, like Woolson, Philip is not overfond of society.

Philip's and Gertrude's antagonist is Philip's wife, Amy, a woman devoted to beauty and social occasion, a vestigial representative of the domestic beauty and Cult of True Womanhood of earlier in the century. The wires attached to the wings of the angel of the house, however, are now visible: "At present her beauty was gone; in appearance she was insignificant. Her small figure was wasted, her little face was pallid, her blue eyes had lost their bright color, and the golden hair had grown ominously thin" (474). Amy's primary trait is selfishness. She encourages her husband to be more productive and to contract himself to a syndicate—to prefer quantity to quality in his own work—and to move from his country estate with its large library to Washington so that his wife can enjoy the social whirl. Much to her husband's dismay, she also pressures Philip to change the family's reservations for their return passage to America from one ocean line to another. Whether her reason for changing the family's reservations is dictated by whim, class consciousness, jealousy over Philip's and Gertrude's shared literary interest, or the desire to exercise petty power, the reader can only imagine. At the end of the narrative we learn that indeed the family has booked passage on Amy's choice of line and that they have closed the country estate. The implication, of course, is that Philip will also abandon his artistic standards, become associated with a syndicate, and write novels designed for general consumption, like Gray Tucker's uncomplicated books that make people laugh. Amy's very name suggests her function in the narrative. She is *aimée,* beloved, but as the English spelling suggests with its inclusion of *-my,* the personal possessive form, it implies that she and her values are self-centered and self-serving.

Yet Amy represents the cultural norm. Although her beauty has faded, she (and the women's culture world of which she is a part) dominates and is pampered. Her wishes to travel by the White Star Line rather than by Cunard, and to move from London to Washington, are granted. Unlike Marion Carroll, she will deny herself nothing. The "Me" and "My" generation of the period, complete with its commercial devotion, has negated artistic efforts. And Amy is evidently teaching her daughter, Polly, the ways of her world, for she, too is guilty of selfishness, though in a genuinely childish way.

In such a world where commercialism and selfishness rule, Gertrude is an oddity. As Amy says, "You spinsters are too queer. You are either so prudish that one can't look at you, or else you're so emancipated that Heaven alone knows what you'll say next! It all comes from your ignorance, I suppose" (475). Philip considers Gertrude's devotion to George Eliot, a female writer, "absurd." Nine years older than Amy, the spinster recognizes the drift of the future as it becomes more and more obvious to her through her reading. As she notes,

> "I had happened to read the *Life of Louisa Alcott* just before I began the Bashkirtseff journal. . . . What a contrast! It is true that the Russian girl was but twenty-four when she died, but one feels that she would have been the same at fifty. Miss Alcott worked all her life as hard as she possibly could, turning her hand to anything that offered, no matter what; and her sole motive was to assist her parents and her family, those who were dear to her; of

herself she never thought at all. Marie Bashkirtseff's behavior to her mother and aunt showed indifference, and often scorn; her one thought was herself—her own attractions, her own happiness, her own celebrity, and the persons who could perhaps add to the latter two. Her egotism—" (475)

The artistry of self-sacrifice, Gertrude realizes, is a relic of the past: Bashkirtseff and self-indulgence are the waves of the future. She also realizes that she herself is considered absurd. Perhaps Woolson, too, felt out of place in a changing world. In any case, the art Woolson had recognized as valid and valued is now, in an increasingly commercial world, outmoded. Even Gertrude, her sensitive, talented spinster, does not keep a diary. And although she has apparently sacrificed her life for the Moore family, she (and her admiration of George Eliot) is considered ridiculous rather than, like Marion Carroll, generous.

The concluding paragraph of the story suggests that Woolson recognized the limited possibilities of art in the new century. The Moores' New Edinburgh country home and its large library are compromised by the growing emphasis on commercial endeavor, as the intermittent references to stock prices reflect. "Gertrude Remington does not keep a diary. But in a small almanac she jots down occasional brief notes. This is one of them: 'New Edinburgh, February 20, 1892. Philip and A. gone to Washington. House here closed'" (478). Gertrude's values, and by extension, Woolson's own—art, loyalty, self-sacrifice, hard work—were no longer validated by society. The fin de siècle also signaled a *fin de valeur:* a shift away from the world that had preceded, the sense we have in other end-of-the-century narratives, such as Kate Chopin's *The Awakening,* a work written seven years after "In Sloane Street."

The woman writer, according to Judith Kegan Gardiner, sees herself in her protagonist, especially if that protagonist is female.[6] Gardiner's observation seems to apply especially to artist-heroine fiction not only in the nineteenth but also in the twentieth century, as a work like Sylvia Plath's *The Bell Jar* demonstrates. In many ways Constance Fenimore Woolson is, in turn, each of her heroines. Like Miss Elisabetha and Catherine, the painter of "Felipa," she is devoted to her young relations. As she wrote to her nephew, Samuel Mather, on 8

February 1892, rather late in her life, "It is only through nephews & nieces, & now grandnephews & niece if you please, that I keep in touch with the actual life of the day" (Mather Family Papers). Like the heroine of *Anne,* Woolson is an active walker and rower and an educated botanist. Like Aaronna Moncrief, Woolson and other women of the age approach celebrated writers for help in getting their own pieces into print. With Henry James, Woolson tours the galleries of Europe, as her heroine Ettie Macks does with Raymond Noel. Woolson admires Mme de Staël as Katharine Winthrop does. And Woolson shares with Marion Carroll a distrust of the clergy. Finally, like Prudence Wilkin, Woolson throughout her life identifies herself as a New Englander, and like Gertrude Remington, she sees herself as an independent woman caught in a predicament: a spinster, or, as she calls herself, "a solitary old bird," inhabiting a shifting middle ground between what her antagonist Amy Moore perceives as extremes.

Woolson's artist-heroines speak for her, addressing the dilemma of loss: of tradition, of role models, of identity. Their "impoverishment," as Ann Douglas Wood calls it, is one of instability and silence.[7] Critical comment on Woolson has always assigned her other voices. In her own day one critic, to whom Woolson was doubtless indebted for comparing her to her own literary heroine, wrote that "a fragment, and not an inferior fragment, of the mantle of George Eliot is resting on her capable shoulders."[8] In our day Leon Edel has made Woolson into a weak echo of James. Woolson's originality has always been read in light of the anxiety of literary influence. Few have ever identified in her an individual, original voice tied to a single distinctive landscape, two traditional criteria for literary merit.

Indeed, one can only agree that Woolson is a sort of literary vagabond, lacking identification with one geographical locale in the way that, say, Sarah Orne Jewett is associated with Maine, Willa Cather with Nebraska, or Eudora Welty with Mississippi. Undoubtedly, Woolson's wandering through England, Europe, and the Middle East made her feel rootless and curiously homesick for the home she did not have. Just two years before her death, she invented a plan to provide some stability in her life, describing it on 8 February 1892 to Samuel Mather:

But, do you know, Sam—I *have* a plan. It is vague. But still it is more of a plan than any I have had for ten years. I have long hoped (as you know) to go to housekeeping again, in Venice. Lately the idea has come to me that before I do that, I'll go home for a year. I want to see all of you at Cleveland, first of all. Then I should like once more to see Mackinac. Then a few days at Cooperstown for Mother's sake. Then a winter in Florida. After that, it will be time enough for Venice. I have set no dates for all this. Because first, as a standing-point, I wish to do a certain amount of literary work.—Nothing less could possibly content me. I am hoping that my health will improve. And all the doctors say that it will. They all, however, advise me to live in a warm climate. (Mather Family Papers)

She did not, however, make that trip, unlike her friend Henry James, whose tour of America in 1905 resulted in the essays collected in *The American Scene.* Instead, a request she had made in her sorrow over her brother's death ten years before her own came to pass. In a letter dated 16 January 1884, she had asked her nephew to ensure her own burial in Europe should she die there (Mather Family Papers).

Both identity and the power that attends it are denied Woolson's artist-heroines by the patriarchal culture in which they exist. Like the narrator of "'Miss Grief,'" however, we must admit the power of the spinster and of her fictions, her other selves. "You had success," she whispers to the narrator on her death bed, "—but I had the greater power."[9] The grief of Aaronna Moncrief's artistry is that the male establishment, in order to protect its own interests, withholds her work from the public. At the conclusion of "'Miss Grief,'" the narrator admits, "I never knew more of her history than is written here. If there was more that I might have learned, it remained unlearned, for I did not ask."[10]

This study begins to ask just those questions whose responses will reconstruct the history of Constance Fenimore Woolson and interpret the grief of her artistry—and that of other women of her generation.

NOTES

INTRODUCTION

1. Clare Benedict, ed., *Constance Fenimore Woolson*, vol. 2 of *Five Generations (1785–1923)* (London: Ellis, 1930), p. 25.

2. Alfred Habegger, *Gender, Fantasy, and Realism in American Literature* (New York: Columbia University Press, 1982), p. 105.

3. Elaine Showalter, "Feminist Criticism in the Wilderness," in *The New Feminist Criticism: Essays on Women, Literature, and Theory* (New York: Pantheon, 1985), p. 259.

4. Letter to E. C. Stedman, 23 July 1876, Edmund C. Stedman Papers, Rare Book and Manuscript Library, Columbia University. (Hereafter cited parenthetically within the text as Stedman Papers.) I am grateful for permission to quote from these letters.

ONE • TRADITIONS OF ARTISTRY AND GENDER

1. Lyon N. Richardson, "Constance Fenimore Woolson, 'Novelist Laureate' of America," *South Atlantic Quarterly* 39 (1940): 29.

2. Helen Gray Cone, "Women in American Literature," *Century Magazine* 40 (1890): 927.

3. Jay B. Hubbell, *The South in American Literature: 1607–1900* (Durham: Duke University Press, 1954), pp. 735, 726.

4. See, for example, Henry Mills Alden, *Harper's Weekly* 38 (3 February 1894): 113–114; *New York Times*, 27 January 1894, p. 10; and Margaret E. Sangster, *Harper's Bazar* 27 (3 February 1894): 93–94.

5. Fred Lewis Pattee, *The Development of the American Short Story: An Historical Survey* (New York: Harper and Brothers, 1923), pp. 250, 254.

6. Arthur Hobson Quinn, *American Fiction: An Historical Survey* (New York: D. Appleton-Century Company, 1936), p. 342.

7. Alexander Cowie, *The Rise of the American Novel* (New York: American Book Company, 1948), p. 568.

8. John Dwight Kern, *Constance Fenimore Woolson: Literary Pioneer* (Philadelphia: University of Pennsylvania Press, 1934) and Rayburn S. Moore, *Constance Fenimore Woolson* (New York: Twayne, 1963).

9. Richardson, "Constance Fenimore Woolson," 32.

10. Evelyn Thomas Helmick, "Constance Fenimore Woolson: First Novelist of Florida," in *Feminist Criticism: Essays on Theory, Poetry and Prose*, ed. Cheryl L. Brown and Karen Olson (Metuchen, N.J.: Scarecrow Press, 1978), p. 238.

11. See Nancy F. Cott, *The Bonds of Womanhood: Woman's Sphere in New England, 1780–1835* (New Haven: Yale University Press, 1977) and Carroll Smith-Rosenberg, "The Female World of Love and Ritual: Relations Between Women in Nineteenth-Century America," in *The Signs Reader: Women, Gender and Scholarship*, ed. Elizabeth Abel and Emily K. Abel (Chicago: University of Chicago Press, 1983), pp. 27–55.

12. Nina Baym, *Woman's Fiction: A Guide to Novels by and About Women in America, 1820–1870* (Ithaca: Cornell University Press, 1978), p. 22.

13. Carolyn Forrey, "The New Woman Revisited," *Women's Studies* 2 (1972): 39.

14. Ibid.

15. Ann Douglas Wood, "The Literature of Impoverishment: The Women Local Colorists in America, 1865–1914," *Women's Studies* 1 (1972): 12–13.

16. Judith Fetterley, introduction to *Provisions: A Reader from Nineteenth-Century American Women* (Bloomington: Indiana University Press, 1985), p. 15.

17. Leon Edel, *The Middle Years: 1882–1895*, vol. 3 of *The Life of Henry James* (1962; rpt., New York: Avon Books, 1978), p. 203.

18. See Josephine Donovan, *New England Local Color Literature: A Women's Tradition* (New York: Frederick Ungar, 1983), and Wood, "Literature of Impoverishment," 3–45.

19. Catharine Sedgwick, "Cacoethes Scribendi," in *Provisions: A Reader from Nineteenth-Century American Women*, ed. Judith Fetterley (Bloomington: Indiana University Press, 1985), p. 59.

20. Kate Chopin, *The Awakening*, ed. Margaret Culley (New York: W. W. Norton, 1976), p. 82.

21. Judith Kegan Gardiner, "On Female Identity and Writing by Women," *Writing and Sexual Difference*, ed. Elizabeth Abel (Chicago: University of Chicago Press, 1982), p. 187.

22. Gardiner, "On Female Identity," p. 179.

23. Alice Hall Petry, "'Always, Your Attached Friend': The Unpublished Letters of Constance Fenimore Woolson to John and Clara Hay," *Books at Brown* 29–30 (1982–1983): 12.

24. Edel, *The Middle Years*, p. 363.

25. Ibid., p. 87.

26. Ibid., p. 88.

27. Ibid., p. 203.

28. Ibid., p. 204.

29. Henry James, review of *Dallas Galbraith* by Rebecca Harding Davis, in *Literary Criticism: Essays on Literature, American, English Writers* (New York: Library of America, 1984), p. 223.

30. Henry James, *Henry James Letters*, vol. 3 (1883–1895), ed. Leon Edel (Cambridge, Mass.: Belknap Press, 1980), p. 151.

31. Henry James, "Miss Woolson," in *Literary Criticism: Essays on Literature, American, English Writers* (New York: Library of America, 1984), p. 639.

32. Jean Strouse, *Alice James: A Biography* (Boston: Houghton Mifflin Company, 1980), pp. 312–313.

33. Ibid., p. 260.

34. Ibid., p. 260.

35. Ibid., p. 259.

36. Edel, *The Middle Years*, p. 215.

37. *Henry James Letters*, 3:153.

38. Ibid., 3:165. After the mid-1870s, Woolson became increasingly deaf and was finally forced to rely on an ear trumpet.

39. Ibid., 3:246, 249.

40. Ibid., 3:382.

41. Ibid., 3:436–437.

42. Ibid., 3:xvi.

43. Ibid., 3:542.

44. I found Woolson's personal copy of this text in the Woolson House on the Rollins College campus in Winter Park, Florida. I am indebted to the Rollins College Department of Special Collections, College Archives, and Records Management for permission to use this and other items in the Woolson Collection of Memorabilia.

45. Epictetus, *The Teaching of Epictetus,* trans. T. W. Rolleston (New York: Thomas Whittaker, 1888), p. 135.

46. Epictetus, *Teaching,* p. 200.

47. Permission to quote from Woolson's letters to her nephew and his wife, Samuel and Flora Mather, and to her niece, Katherine Mather, collected in the Mather Family Papers, MSS. 3735, has been granted by the Western Reserve Historical Society, Cleveland, Ohio. Further letters are noted parenthetically within the text as Mather Family Papers. In citing Woolson's letters, I have retained her idiosyncratic spelling and punctuation, notably the misplaced apostrophe in contractions.

48. Clare Benedict, ed., *Voices out of the Past,* vol. 1 of *Five Generations (1785–1923)* (London: Ellis, 1930), p. 244.

49. Clare Benedict, ed., *Constance Fenimore Woolson,* vol. 2 of *Five Generations (1785–1923)* (London: Ellis, 1930), p. 52.

50. Jack Fincher, "Notice: Sunlight May Be Necessary for Your Health," *Smithsonian* 16 (1985): 72.

51. Elaine Showalter, *A Literature of Their Own: British Women Novelists from Brontë to Lessing* (Princeton, N.J.: Princeton University Press, 1977), p. 194.

52. Edel, *The Middle Years,* pp. 377, 385.

53. Leon Edel, *The Conquest of London: 1870–1881,* vol. 2 of *The Life of Henry James* (1962; rpt., New York: Avon Books, 1978), p. 417.

54. Sharon Dean, "Constance Fenimore Woolson and Henry James: The Literary Relationship," *Massachusetts Studies in English* 7 (1980): 1.

55. Dean, "Woolson and Henry James," 1–8.

TWO • A WOMAN WRITER BORN MIDCENTURY

1. For an extended definition of True Womanhood, see Barbara Welter, "The Cult of True Womanhood: 1820–1860," *American Quarterly* 18 (1966): 151–174. The figure of the New Woman is also treated in Carolyn Forrey, "The New Woman Revisited," *Women's Studies* 2 (1972): 37–56.

2. Sandra M. Gilbert and Susan Gubar, eds., *The Norton Anthology of Literature by Women* (New York: W. W. Norton, 1985).

3. Welter, "Cult of True Womanhood," 151, n. 1.

4. Ibid., p. 152.

5. See Carroll Smith-Rosenberg, "The Female World of Love and Ritual: Relations Between Women in Nineteenth-Century America," in *The Signs Reader: Women, Gender and Scholarship,* ed. Elizabeth Abel and Emily K. Abel (Chicago: University of Chicago Press, 1983), pp. 27–55.

6. Joan Myers Weimer, "Women Artists as Exiles in the Fiction of Constance Fenimore Woolson," *Legacy* 3 (1986): 4, asserts that because of Woolson's tragic loss of her siblings, she was "cautious of all attachments, and wary of marriage." Woolson's younger brother, Charlie, died in California in circumstances that suggest suicide. In a letter on black-bordered stationery to Samuel Mather dated 16 January [1884], Woolson writes that she has been ill: "I presume all came from the shock of Charlie's death,—which made me suffer more than I have ever suffered in my life. I was so extremely unhappy for a number of weeks that I did not know where to turn. Charley left behind a letter, or rather two—a sort of diary—which he had written at different times during the summer. The diary showed suffering so piteous that it broke my heart. I cannot imagine any suffering greater than his was, at the last. I will say no more. I know you were sincerely attached to him; & to all your family, he was most grateful, for the kind acts which gave the only gleam of pleasure he had, during those last years. This diary of his only reached me, of course, after his death. I have destroyed it, as he requested. Strange and mysterious are the ties of blood. I had seen so little of Charlie since he grew to be a man; we had been separated for so many years; & yet his death—out there in California—has made me perfectly desolate" (Mather Family Papers).

7. Much of my information regarding Woolson's early life is condensed from Rayburn S. Moore, *Constance Fenimore Woolson* (New York: Twayne, 1963), pp. 18–24.

8. Benedict, ed., *Constance Fenimore Woolson,* vol. 2 of *Five Generations (1785–1923)* (London: Ellis, 1930), p. 19.

9. Ibid., pp. 17–18.

10. Constance Fenimore Woolson, "The Haunted Lake," *Harper's New Monthly Magazine* 44 (December 1871): 20–30.

11. Various photographs and other memorabilia are on display at Woolson House on the Rollins College campus, Winter Park, Florida.

12. Benedict, ed., *Constance Fenimore Woolson,* pp. 111–112.

13. Forrey, "New Woman Revisited," pp. 38–39.

14. Benedict, ed., *Constance Fenimore Woolson,* p. 18.

15. Ibid., p. 49.

16. Ibid., p. 99.

17. Ibid., p. 27.

18. Moore, *Constance Fenimore Woolson,* pp. 21–22.

19. Jay B. Hubbell, "Some New Letters of Constance Fenimore Woolson," *New England Quarterly* 14 (1941): 726.

20. Anne March, *The Old Stone House* (Boston: D. Lothrop and Company, 1872).

21. Benedict, ed., *Constance Fenimore Woolson,* p. 20.

22. Ibid., p. 20.

23. Ibid., pp. 21–22.

24. Ibid., pp. 126, 128, 141.

25. Ibid., pp. 134, 136, 137, 140, 144, 149.

26. Jay Hubbell, "Some New Letters of Constance Fenimore Woolson," p. 729.

27. Henry James, "Miss Woolson," *Literary Criticism: Essays on Literature, American, English Writers* (New York: Library of America, 1984), p. 649.

28. James, "Miss Woolson," pp. 639–640.

29. Henry James, *Henry James Letters,* vol. 3 (1883–1895), ed. Leon Edel (Cambridge, Mass.: Belknap Press, 1980), p. 544. Woolson writes: "I am sorry that I said anything to you of my small success in *Anne,* at home. When your answer came, I was vexed that I had. At the time I was writing you, I was in a state of surprise over a letter from the Messrs. Harper voluntarily doubling the sum they had already paid me for the story, and also proposing to give me a liberal percent on the sale in book form,—a thing expressly denied me in the original sale of the MS. This struck me as so remarkable that I mentioned it to you. But of course you understood that what is great success to me, would be nothing to you. All the money that I have received, and shall receive, from my long novel, does not equal probably the half of the sum you received for your first, or shortest."

30. Ibid., 3:528.

THREE • *ANNE:* WOOLSON'S PORTRAIT OF A LADY

1. Mary Kelley, *Private Woman, Public Stage* (New York: Oxford University Press, 1984) and Nina Baym, *Woman's Fiction: Novels by and About Women in America* (Ithaca: Cornell University Press, 1978).

2. Constance Fenimore Woolson, "Duets," *Harper's New Monthly Magazine* 49 (September 1874): 579–585.

3. Constance Fenimore Woolson, "Weighed in the Balance," *Appleton's Journal* 7 (1 June 1872): 590.

4. Constance Fenimore Woolson, *Castle Nowhere: Lake Country Sketches* (Boston: J. R. Osgood and Company, 1875).

5. Constance Fenimore Woolson, *Anne* (New York: Harper and Brothers, 1882). Page numbers are cited parenthetically within the text.

6. Henry James, *The Portrait of a Lady,* ed. Robert D. Bamberg (New

York: W. W. Norton, 1975). I have chosen to use the Norton Critical Edition since it offers a list of textual variants from the first edition of 1881 in addition to the text of the later New York edition. Because the 1908 edition differs from the original, written while Woolson was at work on *Anne,* the reader should consult the 1881 first edition variants, as I have done. Page numbers are cited parenthetically within the text.

7. Alfred Habegger refers to Henry James and William Dean Howells as sissies in chapter 7 of *Gender, Fantasy, and Realism in American Literature* (New York: Columbia University Press, 1982), pp. 56–65.

8. Baym, *Woman's Fiction,* p. 22.

9. Carren Kaston, *Imagination and Desire in the Novels of Henry James* (New Brunswick, N.J.: Rutgers University Press, 1984), p. 40.

10. Habegger, *Gender, Fantasy,* p. 56.

11. Kaston, *Imagination and Desire,* p. 41.

12. Ibid., p. 41.

13. Ibid., p. 41.

14. William Veeder, *Henry James—The Lessons of the Master: Popular Fiction and Personal Style in the Nineteenth Century* (Chicago: University of Chicago Press, 1975), p. 71.

15. Veeder, *Henry James,* p. 120.

16. For the idea of the resisting reader, I am indebted to Judith Fetterley, *The Resisting Reader: A Feminist Approach to American Fiction* (Bloomington: Indiana University Press, 1978).

17. Joyce Warren, *The American Narcissus: Individualism and Women in Nineteenth-Century Fiction* (New Brunswick, N.J.: Rutgers University Press, 1984), pp. 43, 49.

18. Kaston, *Imagination and Desire,* p. 40.

19. Henry James, *Henry James Letters,* vol. 3 (1883–1895), ed. Leon Edel (Cambridge, Mass.: Belknap Press, 1980), p. 535.

20. See Baym, *Woman's Fiction,* and Kelley, *Private Woman.*

21. *Henry James Letters,* 3:544–545.

22. For extensive discussions of how women's writing empowers its female readers, see for example, Baym, *Woman's Fiction,* and Kelley, *Private Woman.*

23. *Anne* was published by Harper and Brothers in 1882, 1903, and 1910, and by Sampson and Low (London) in 1883. The Arno Press has reprinted the Harper's text with a new introduction by Elizabeth Hardwick.

24. Judith Kegan Gardiner, "On Female Identity and Writing by Women," in *Writing and Sexual Difference,* ed. Elizabeth Abel (Chicago: University of Chicago Press, 1982), p. 187.

25. Ellen Moers, *Literary Women: The Great Writers* (1976: rpt., New York: Oxford University Press, 1985), p. 130.

26. Annis Pratt, *Archetypal Patterns in Women's Fiction* (Bloomington: Indiana University Press, 1981), p. 21.

27. I located a list of wildflowers Woolson had seen, written in the back cover of a wildflower text in the holdings of the Olin Library at Rollins College, Winter Park, Florida, where I also found two unpublished Woolson poems, "Ferns" and "Fern Fragments," tucked in the back of a book.

28. James, "Miss Woolson," *Literary Criticism: Essays on Literature, American, English Writers* (New York: Library of America, 1984), p. 642.

29. Sandra M. Gilbert and Susan Gubar, *The Madwoman in the Attic: The Woman Writer and the Nineteenth-Century Literary Imagination* (New Haven: Yale University Press, 1979), pp. 77–78.

30. Ibid., p. 249.

31. Moers, *Literary Women*, p. 1.

FOUR • "MISS ELISABETHA" AND "FELIPA": ARTISTRY IN THE DOMESTIC SPHERE

1. Constance Fenimore Woolson, *Rodman the Keeper: Southern Sketches* (1880; rpt., New York: Harper and Brothers, 1886). Some critics turn to this collection as evidence for their assertions that Woolson's best writing is done on the timely topic of the Civil War, an event that touched her—and everyone else's—life. Her sympathetic tone continues to be much remarked, and readers note that Woolson had a soldier boyfriend, a captain in the Union Army, who returned from action a changed man. More recent feminist critics, however, agree that Woolson's artist-heroine fiction is more interesting and complex.

2. The term *wild zone* I adapt from Elaine Showalter's discussion of the research of Edwin and Shirley Ardener on the Bakweri people of Cameroon. In the Bakweri culture women participate in both the dominant and a muted culture. The wild zone is the metaphoric space in which the muted women's culture exists. See Showalter's "Feminist Criticism in the Wilderness," in *The New Feminist Criticism: Essays on Women, Literature, and Theory* (New York: Pantheon, 1985), p. 262.

3. Isabel Hill, trans., *Corinne, or Italy* by Madame de Staël (New York: A. L. Burt, n.d.), p. xiii.

4. Madame de Staël, *Corinne, or Italy*, trans. Isabel Hill (New York: A. L. Burt, n.d.), p. 24.

5. Ibid., p. 236.

6. Ibid., pp. 233–234.

7. Ellen Moers, *Literary Women: The Great Writers* (1976; rpt., New York: Oxford University Press, 1985), pp. 173–210.

8. George Sand, *Lélia,* trans. Maria Espinosa (Bloomington: Indiana University Press, 1978), pp. 116–117.

9. Ibid., p. 74.

10. Elizabeth Barrett Browning, *Aurora Leigh* (Chicago: Academy Chicago Limited, 1979).

11. Louisa May Alcott, *Diana and Persis,* ed. Sarah Elbert (New York: Arno Press, 1978), p. 127.

12. Ibid., p. 65.

13. Barrett Browning, *Aurora Leigh,* p. 10.

14. Elizabeth Stuart Phelps, *The Story of Avis,* ed. Carol Farley Kessler (New Brunswick, N.J.: Rutgers University Press, 1985), p. 30.

15. Ibid., p. 64, 107.

16. See Catherine Sedgwick, "Cacoethes Scribendi," in *Provisions: A Reader from Nineteenth-Century American Women,* ed. Judith Fetterley (Bloomington: Indiana University Press, 1985), pp. 41–59; and Sarah Payson Willis, *Fern Leaves from Fanny's Portfolio* (Auburn, N.Y.: Derby and Miller, 1853), pp. 100–104.

17. Maurice Beebe, *Ivory Towers and Sacred Founts: The Artist as Hero in Fiction From Goethe to Joyce* (New York: New York University Press, 1964).

18. The preceding taxonomy is condensed from Linda Huf, *A Portrait of the Artist as a Young Woman* (New York: Frederick Ungar, 1983), pp. 4–11.

19. Ibid., pp. 10–11.

20. Grace Stewart, *A New Mythos: The Novel of the Artist as Heroine: 1877–1977* (Brattleboro, Vt.: Eden Press Women's Publications, Inc., 1979), p. 14.

21. Ibid., p. 175.

22. Ibid., pp. 175–176, 177, 178.

23. Constance Fenimore Woolson, "Miss Elisabetha," in *Rodman the Keeper: Southern Sketches* (1880; rpt., New York: Harper and Brothers, 1886), pp. 75–104. Hereafter page references are cited parenthetically within the text.

24. Constance Fenimore Woolson, "Felipa," in *Rodman the Keeper: Southern Sketches* (1880; rpt., New York: Harper and Brothers, 1886), pp. 197–220. Hereafter page references are cited parenthetically within the text.

25. Lee R. Edwards, "The Labors of Psyche: Toward a Theory of Female Heroism," *Critical Inquiry* 6 (1979): 48.

FIVE • "'MISS GRIEF'": THE GRIEF OF ARTISTRY

1. Alice Hall Petry, "'Always, Your Attached Friend': The Unpublished Letters of Constance Fenimore Woolson to John and Clara Hay," *Books at Brown* 29–30 (1982–1983): 31–32.

2. Ibid., p. 102.

3. Constance Fenimore Woolson, "'Miss Grief,'" *Lippincott's Magazine* 25 (May 1880): 574–585. Page numbers cited parenthetically within the text, however, correspond to those in Constance Fenimore Woolson, *For the Major and Selected Short Stories,* ed. Rayburn S. Moore (New Haven: College and University Press Publishers, 1967), pp. 123–143.

4. John Dwight Kern, *Constance Fenimore Woolson: Literary Pioneer* (Philadelphia: University of Pennsylvania Press, 1934), p. 117.

5. Ibid., p. 117.

6. Sharon Dean, "Constance Fenimore Woolson and Henry James: The Literary Relationship," *Massachusetts Studies in English* 7 (1980): 7.

7. Ibid., 6, 8.

8. Leon Edel, *The Conquest of London: 1870–1881,* vol. 2 of *The Life of Henry James* (1962; rpt., New York: Avon Books, 1978), p. 417.

9. Rayburn S. Moore, *Constance Fenimore Woolson* (New York: Twayne, 1963), p. 156, n. 27.

10. The most recent reprinting of "'Miss Grief'" appeared in *Legacy* 4 (1987): 13–25. As this study goes to press, the Rutgers University Press plans to publish *Women Artists, Women Exiles: "'Miss Grief'" and Other Stories,* ed. Joan Myers Weimer.

11. The narrator's servant, Simpson, and his fiancée, Isabel, though members of the underclass, do identify with the narrator, in fact, adopting his class status by joking with him about Miss Grief and by marrying him, respectively.

12. I quote from the King James text of the Bible.

13. C. G. Rossetti, *Seek and Find,* cited in the OED definition of *Aaronic.*

14. Henry L. Reynolds, *John the Baptist,* cited in the OED definition of *Aaronic.*

15. Florence Nightingale, *Cassandra* (Old Westbury, N.Y.: The Feminist Press, 1979), p. 53.

16. Even at this early point the narrator hints at his fear of strong women,

like Tullia and Lucrezia Borgia, who destroy the men they touch. (Later we learn that he likes his women weak, narrow, and dependent, like Isabel Abercrombie.) His implicit deprecation of them, while allowing him further control of the interview with the insistent Miss Grief, serves an ironic (Aaronic) purpose; for Miss Grief will prove as powerful as the women whose possessions the narrator thinks she represents even though, in another ironic twist, she, not he, is destroyed.

17. The narrator's fiancée is named *Ethelind* in the original *Lippincott's* text. Her name may have been changed to *Isabel* in a later version to differentiate her from Ethelinda Faith Macks, Woolson's artist-heroine in "The Street of the Hyacinth" (1882).

18. *Vixenish* appears in the original *Lippincott's* version. In the reprint I cite, however, the adjective is changed to *murky.*

19. See, for example, Robin Lakoff, *Language and Woman's Place* (New York: Harper and Row, 1975).

20. Ursula Le Guin, "She Unnames Them," *The New Yorker,* 21 January 1985, 27.

21. As students in my American Women Writers course pointed out to me, the narrator is more vampiric than one might expect on first reading. Should Aaronna Moncrief's work remain in his possession, it would become, on his death, part of his literary remains. Given his fame, her work might well be attributed to him, enabling the narrator, rather than Miss Grief, to live on in vampiric fashion.

22. Eugene Exman, *The House of Harper: One Hundred and Fifty Years of Publishing* (New York: Harper and Row, 1967), p. 78.

SIX • REWRITING MADAME DE STAËL: WOOLSON'S "AT THE CHÂTEAU OF CORINNE"

1. Clare Benedict, ed., *Constance Fenimore Woolson,* vol. 2 of *Five Generations (1785–1923)* (London: Ellis, 1930), p. 226.

2. As Ellen Moers notes, because the public so closely identified Mme de Staël's colorful life with Corinne's, the latter's name came to stand for both the historical figure and her creation, *Literary Women: The Great Writers* (1976; rpt., New York: Oxford University Press, 1985), p. 176.

3. Moers, *Literary Women,* p. 173.

4. Madelyn Gutwirth, *Madame de Staël, Novelist: The Emergence of the Artist as Woman* (Urbana: University of Illinois Press, 1978), p. 211.

5. Gutwirth, *Madame de Staël,* p. 207.

6. John Dwight Kern, *Constance Fenimore Woolson: Literary Pioneer* (Philadelphia: University of Pennsylvania Press, 1934), p. 140; Arthur Hobson Quinn, *American Fiction: An Historical Survey* (New York: American Book Company, 1948), p. 342.

7. Rayburn S. Moore, *Constance Fenimore Woolson* (New York: Twayne, 1963), p. 74.

8. Constance Fenimore Woolson, "At the Château of Corinne," in *Dorothy and Other Italian Stories* (New York: Harper and Brothers, 1896), pp. 237–287. Page references are cited parenthetically within the text.

9. Gutwirth, *Madame de Staël,* p. 204.

10. Moers, *Literary Women,* p. 173.

11. Ibid., p. 175.

12. Sandra M. Gilbert and Susan Gubar, *The Madwoman in the Attic: The Woman Writer and the Nineteenth-Century Literary Imagination* (New Haven: Yale University Press, 1979).

13. Moers, *Literary Women,* p. 244.

14. J. E. Cirlot, *A Dictionary of Symbols,* 2d ed., trans. Jack Sage (New York: Philosophical Library, 1983), p. 112.

15. See Linda Huf, *A Portrait of the Artist as a Young Woman* (New York: Frederick Ungar, 1983), p. 9, for a discussion of the figure of the Eternal Masculine in the woman's *Künstlerroman.*

16. Cirlot, *Dictionary of Symbols,* p. 172.

17. Jean Baker Miller, *Toward a New Psychology of Women* (Boston: Beacon Press, 1976), pp. 122–123.

18. Gutwirth, *Madame de Staël,* pp. 255–256.

19. Huf, *Portrait of the Artist,* p. 9.

20. Luce Irigaray, *Speculum of the Other Woman,* trans. Gillian C. Gill (Ithaca: Cornell University Press, 1985), p. 94. My quotations from Irigaray derive from her discussion of anal-eroticism, a component of John Ford's narcissistic personality.

21. Ibid., p. 94.

22. Ibid., p. 95.

23. Gilbert and Gubar, *The Madwoman in the Attic,* p. 37.

24. Henry James, "Modern Women," *Literary Criticism: Essays on Literature, American, English Writers* (New York: Library of America, 1984), p. 22.

25. Benedict, ed., *Constance Fenimore Woolson,* p. 300.

26. Ibid., p. 304.

27. Ibid.

28. Sandra M. Gilbert, "From *Patria* to *Matria:* Elizabeth Barrett Browning's *Risorgimento,*" *PMLA* 99 (1984): 197.

29. Benedict, ed., *Constance Fenimore Woolson,* p. 47.

SEVEN • "THE STREET OF THE HYACINTH": THE CONVENTIONS OF FAITH

1. Constance Fenimore Woolson, "The Street of the Hyacinth," in *The Front Yard and Other Italian Stories* (New York: Harper and Brothers, 1895), pp. 137–193. My parenthetical page references, however, follow the more accessible text reprinted in Constance Fenimore Woolson, *For the Major and Selected Short Stories,* ed. Rayburn S. Moore, (New Haven: College and University Press, 1967), pp. 144–183. Moore, in *Constance Fenimore Woolson* (New York: Twayne, 1963), pronounces the story "a good piece of work" (p. 68); Sharon Dean declares it "not entirely successful," "Constance Fenimore Woolson and Henry James: The Literary Relationship," *Massachusetts Studies in English* 7 (1980): 4.

2. Moore, *Constance Fenimore Woolson,* p. 68.

3. Dean, "Woolson and Henry James," 3.

4. Ibid., 4.

5. *L'écriture féminine,* woman's writing, is a French feminist concept used to describe the writing deriving from a system that rejects patriarchally structured and dictated language. See, for example, Ann Rosalind Jones, "Writing the Body: Toward an Understanding of *l'Écriture féminine,*" *The New Feminist Criticism: Essays on Women, Literature, and Theory,* ed. Elaine Showalter (New York: Pantheon, 1985), pp. 361–377.

6. Perhaps a reason Woolson changed the name of the narrator's fiancée from *Ethelind* to *Isabel* in a revision of "'Miss Grief'" is Woolson's belated recognition that, despite the romantic sound of the name, it also carries masculine resonances. On learning that *Ethelinda* means "noble serpent," Woolson would have deemed the name inappropriate for a character designed as a foil to the vast and truly noble Miss Grief.

7. Annis Pratt, *Archetypal Patterns in Women's Fiction* (Bloomington: Indiana University Press, 1981), p. 29.

8. Linda Huf, *A Portrait of the Artist as a Young Woman* (New York: Frederick Ungar, 1983), p. 5.

9. Sandra M. Gilbert and Susan Gubar, *The Madwoman in the Attic: The Woman Writer and the Nineteenth-Century Literary Imagination* (New Haven: Yale University Press, 1979), p. 81.

10. Grace Stewart, *A New Mythos: The Novel of the Artist as Heroine, 1877–1977* (Brattleboro, Vt.: Eden Press Women's Publications, Inc., 1979), p. 41.

11. Clare Benedict, ed., *Voices Out of the Past,* vol. 1 of *Five Generations (1785–1923)* (London: Ellis, 1930), p. 120.

12. Here I again adapt the Ardeners' term *wild zone* to name a figurative space where the muted culture acts in artistic, cultural, religious, or sexual ways the dominant culture cannot comprehend. See Ardener cited in Elaine Showalter, *The New Feminist Criticism: Essays on Women, Literature, and Theory* (New York: Pantheon, 1985), p. 262.

13. Gilbert and Gubar, *The Madwoman in the Attic,* pp. 77–78.

14. Stewart, *New Mythos,* p. 46.

15. Ibid., p. 47.

16. Edwin Ardener, "The 'Problem' Revisited," *Perceiving Women,* ed. Shirley Ardener (New York: Halsted Press, 1978), p. 23.

17. Luce Irigaray, *This Sex Which Is Not One,* trans. Catherine Porter (Ithaca: Cornell University Press, 1985), p. 127.

18. Dean, "Woolson and Henry James," 4.

19. Moore, *Constance Fenimore Woolson,* p. 67.

20. Ellen Moers, *Literary Women: The Great Writers* (1976; rpt., New York: Oxford University Press, 1985), p. 185.

21. Benedict, ed., *Constance Fenimore Woolson,* vol. 2 of *Five Generations (1785–1923)* (London: Ellis, 1930), pp. 111–112.

EIGHT • *FOR THE MAJOR:* THE ARTISTRY OF GRIEF

1. Henry James, "Miss Woolson," *Literary Criticism: Essays on Literature, American, English Writers* (New York: Library of America, 1984), p. 643.

2. Henry James, "Glasses," *The Complete Tales of Henry James,* vol. 9, ed. Leon Edel (Philadelphia: J. B. Lippincott, 1964), p. 341.

3. Henry James, "Modern Women," *Literary Criticism: Essays on Literature, American, English Writers* (New York: Library of America, 1984), p. 22.

4. Constance Fenimore Woolson, *For the Major* (New York: Harper and Brothers, 1883). Parenthetical page references, however, are to the text reprinted in Constance Fenimore Woolson, *For the Major and Selected Short Stories,* ed. Rayburn S. Moore, (New Haven: College and University Press, 1967), pp. 259–357.

5. Clare Benedict, ed., *Constance Fenimore Woolson,* vol. 2 of *Five Generations (1785–1923)* (London: Ellis, 1930), p. 120.

6. Ann Douglas Wood, "The Literature of Impoverishment: The Women Local Colorists in America 1865–1914," *Women's Studies* 1 (1972): 23.

7. Sybil B. Weir, "Southern Womanhood in the Novels of Constance Fenimore Woolson," *Mississippi Quarterly* 29 (1976): 562, and Nina Baym, *Woman's Fiction: A Guide to Novels by and about Women in America, 1820–1870* (Ithaca: Cornell University Press, 1978), p. 17.

8. Ellen Moers, *Literary Women: The Great Writers* (1976; rpt., New York: Oxford University Press, 1985), p. 255.

9. Wood, "Literature of Impoverishment," 22.

10. Ibid., 22.

11. Old Woman Magoun, the protagonist of the short story of the same name by Mary E. Wilkins Freeman, allows her granddaughter to eat poisonous berries so that the girl will not be taken from her by a marriage to a local gambler.

12. James, "Miss Woolson," p. 643.

13. Sandra M. Gilbert and Susan Gubar, *The Madwoman in the Attic: The Woman Writer and the Nineteenth-Century Literary Imagination* (New Haven: Yale University Press, 1979), p. 615.

14. Ibid., p. 616.

15. Ibid., p. 616.

16. Wood, "Literature of Impoverishment," 22–23; and Weir, "Southern Womanhood," 563.

17. In the elliptical passage the family name is given as Forster. The error of adding or deleting the first *r* is made in the original *Harper's New Monthly Magazine* version (November 1882–April 1883) and has been perpetuated in all printings of the novella.

18. Luce Irigaray, *This Sex Which Is Not One,* trans. Catherine Porter (Ithaca: Cornell University Press, 1985), p. 76.

19. Luce Irigaray, *Speculum of the Other Woman,* trans. Gillian C. Gill (Ithaca: Cornell University Press, 1985), pp. 168–179.

20. Moers, *Literary Women,* p. 244.

21. See Nancy Chodorow, *The Reproduction of Mothering: Psychoanalysis and the Sociology of Gender* (Berkeley: University of California Press, 1978) and Carol Gilligan, *In a Different Voice: Psychological Theory and Women's Development* (Cambridge, Mass.: Harvard University Press, 1982).

22. *Kore,* "the title of the Maiden," is the prototype of Persephone, according to Sir James Frazer, *The Golden Bough: A Study of Magic and Religion* (1922; rpt., New York: Macmillan Company, 1951), p. 488.

23. Luce Irigaray, *Speculum of the Other Woman,* trans. Gillian C. Gill (Ithaca: Cornell University Press, 1985), p. 300.

CONCLUSION

1. Constance Fenimore Woolson, "The Front Yard," in *The Front Yard and Other Italian Stories* (New York: Harper and Brothers, 1895), pp. 1–49. Parenthetical page references, however, are to the text reprinted in Constance Fenimore Woolson, *For the Major and Selected Short Stories,* ed. Rayburn S. Moore (New Haven: College and University Press, 1967), pp. 184–216.

2. Cited in Rayburn S. Moore, *Constance Fenimore Woolson* (New York: Twayne, 1963), p. 62.

3. Rayburn S. Moore, introduction, *For the Major and Selected Short Stories,* p. 18.

4. Constance Fenimore Woolson, "In Sloane Street," *Harper's Bazar,* 25 (11 June 1892): 473–478. Page references are cited parenthetically within the text.

5. Henry James, *Henry James Letters,* vol. 3 (1883–1895), ed. Leon Edel (Cambridge, Mass.: Belknap Press, 1980), p. 528.

6. Judith Kegan Gardiner, "On Female Identity and Writing by Women," *Writing and Sexual Difference,* ed. Elizabeth Abel (Chicago: University of Chicago Press, 1982), p. 187.

7. Ann Douglas Wood, "The Literature of Impoverishment: The Women Local Colorists in America, 1865–1914," *Women's Studies* 1 (1972): 3–45.

8. Alice Hall Petry, "'Always Your Attached Friend': The Unpublished Letters of Constance Fenimore Woolson to John and Clara Hay," *Books at Brown* 29–30 (1982–1983): p. 91, n. 15. Here Petry cites a notice in *Harper's Weekly* 30 (5 June 1886): 366, reprinted from *Century Magazine,* praising Woolson's "insight into the human heart."

9. Constance Fenimore Woolson, "'Miss Grief,'" in *For the Major and Selected Short Stories,* ed. Rayburn S. Moore (New Haven: College and University Press, 1967), p. 142.

10. Ibid., pp. 142–143.

INDEX